Go Such

Strategies for Improving Your Emotional Intelligence

Michael Cornwall PsyD, PhD

DEDICATION

ALBERT "AL" ELLIS (SEPTEMBER 27, 1913 – JULY 24, 2007) was an American psychologist who in 1955 developed rational emotive behavior therapy (REBT). He held M.A. and Ph.D. degrees in clinical psychology from Columbia University and was a member of the American Board of Professional Psychology (ABPP). He founded and was the president emeritus of the New York City–based Albert Ellis Institute. He is generally considered to be the originator of the cognitive revolutionary paradigm shift in psychotherapy and the founder of cognitive–behavioral therapies.

Based on a 1982 professional survey of U.S. and Canadian psychologists, he was considered the second most influential psychotherapist in history. (Carl Rogers ranked first in the survey; Sigmund Freud was ranked third.) Prior to his death, *Psychology Today* described Albert Ellis as the greatest living psychologist.

CONTENTS

Chapter One
Something Truer

I received my undergraduate education in English. I fancied myself a fiction writer, a story-teller. I didn't become a fiction writer, gravitating, instead, into human service and helping, first as social worker, then as a clinical counselor and finally receiving my doctor's degree in health psychology and behavioral medicine.

I often blend my interests in counseling, psychology and fiction writing into the hybrid before you. I am comfortable helping others improve their emotional wellbeing by mixing stories and anecdotes with a little science and philosophy.

＊ ＊ ＊ ＊

Over the course of my early training in psychology, I became particularly interested in psychological theories, of which there are believed to be approximately 700 +. After studying a handful of the more popular philosophies, I narrowed my own interests down to *Rational Emotive Behavior Theory* (REBT). This philosophy of the human mind provided me with personal insight and prepared me to understand *myself*. My interest in Emotional Intelligence theory came later.

* * * *

I attended a conference in Chicago, my last year of graduate school, organized to train new practitioners in the effective and professional use of REBT. While I waited for everyone to be seated, and the conference to get started, I remember hearing a commotion in the back of the room.

"It's him."

"It's Al."

"Look, it's him!"

"That isn't him."

"Yes it is!"

I turned to see a small, very thin and frail man heading up the aisle, carrying a can of juice and a cookie wrapped in cellophane. He didn't really say nor do anything unusual; but everything about him provoked an emotional response in me. Grumpiness wafted after him like dust. He grinned, but his grin was somewhat sinister, boyish. His long nose and horn rimmed glasses made him look unapproachable, yet he shook hands with those who reached out to welcome him, showing a certain measure of enthusiasm and caring.

The man could have passed for a janitor, the guy who adjusts the audio–visual equipment or the president of some small, impoverished eastern European nation. He was no one and everyone, all at the same time. His clothing was disheveled, pants pulled up well past his hips, close to the collar of his shirt, and he was hunched over, as if carrying a huge bundle of kindling in a bunch on his back. He ascended the single step to the stage, carefully shuffled across to his seat and sat down in front of the assembled audience. He paused for a moment, squinting through his glasses at everyone in attendance, as if looking painfully into the sun. He tapped the microphone, pushed his glasses up closer to his eyes, leaned to one side and farted!

"How dreadful!"

"Is this a serious person?"

"What kind of crackpot is this?"

"I told you it wasn't him!"

He continued squinting over his glasses, while inspecting the microphone and looking out over the crowd gathered in his honor. In his nasally New York accent, he groused, "If I have a seizure, someone come up here and feed me this juice," and tapped the tin can with his yellowing fingernail.

It was 1992.

His name was Albert Ellis.

* * * *

Dr. Ellis (who liked to be called Al) was fond of quoting Epictetus, reminding his listeners at every opportunity that *people are disturbed not by things, but by their view of things.* Al is also remembered for his overuse of the word *Fuck*. He used the word in diverse and mixed company as a noun, an adjective, a verb and an adverb. According to Al, "people possess a *fucking* innate human potential for deciding their *fucking* emotions." He stressed that this *innate human potential* was a product of our ability to think about our thinking.

According to Al, the potential for thinking about our thinking is frequently left undeveloped in most people; leaving emotional intelligence unaltered throughout life. Instead of thinking about thinking, we believe, instead, that our emotions are fixed and the product of how events unfold or how we are treated by other people, making emotion something outside our control.

Instead of taking responsibility for our own emotions, Al believed that people choose to whine and complain about how other people should, must, have to and need to change in order for them to be content in their own lives.

Al grumped and groused, "People don't just get upset. They contribute to their own fucking upset–ness. They always have the power to think differently. To think about their thinking. To think about thinking about thinking. Which the goddamn dolphin, as far as we know, can't do. People have much greater ability to change their thinking than any other animal, and I hope that REBT teaches them how to do that."

Al made exaggerated squeaky and whiney sounds to emphasize his points. "There are three *basic musts* that hold us back from our emotional potentials," he said, "First, *I must do well*; secondly, *you must treat me well* and, finally, *my life must always be easy*. We'd better work hard on getting rid of those ideas. We'd better do something about that," he said, "And it will take the force of will to do it!"

* * * *

Over the course of that weekend in Chicago, Al shared his bodily gases and unapologetically used cuss words to describe everything from his childhood, his inability early in life to get a date and his lifetime of precarious physical health. I was thankful for the opportunity, in its entirety, to get to know him.

Later, as a newly–minted therapist from Massachusetts, who had somehow landed in eastern Kentucky, I decided that, in order to practice Al's REBT more authentically, I would have to use the information he gave me about REBT and I would have to say *fuck* as regularly as he did.

No experience left more of an impression on me than when a man and his wife came in for marriage counseling. The man was well over six feet tall, died black hair and blue coveralls. His wife was quite plain, diminutive. Her hair was piled at least a foot in the air, making her seem a bit taller. She stood close to her husband's shoulder, as if relying on its firmness to maintain her balance. There was no sign that there was anything askew in their relationship. They seemed like a particularly well–matched couple.

The man spoke first.

Apparently the judge who was hearing their divorce case directed them to therapy. The man wanted a divorce because men were looking longingly at his wife while she shopped at the grocery store. "It *makes* me angry," he said, looking at his knees. He hinted that the only solution to his problem was divorce. "I can get me someone who no one wants to look at."

After hearing from him, and nothing from his wife, it was my turn to talk. "Thank you for sharing," I said, clearing my throat. "That was a lot to take in."

I have to admit that it was tough for me to generate discussion with this couple. If I asked a question, they looked at each other, shrugged and then looked back at their laps.

No answers.

I talked with the couple about Al's concept of *thinking* and *perception* and how thinking and perception contributed to how we express emotion. "Emotion is a product of *thinking* and *perception*. We have to think and perceive in order to feel emotion. If we want to change the way we feel, we have to change the way we think."

I talked about getting in touch with thoughts and perceptions and how doing that would reveal the subconscious information, the self-talk, we use to draw conclusions about what we are experiencing and the problems we face. "What were you saying to yourself when you noticed men looking at your wife in the grocery store? How were you talking to yourself? What was your self–talk?"

I got no answers; only confused stares.

I talked more about how we can change our thinking by changing our perception and our self–talk. By doing so, we could change our emotions. "We can feel better. We just have to think better," I stressed. "What do you say to yourself when your wife is being observed in the grocery store? We have to get in touch with our thoughts."

The man said, "I don't want to feel better about it."

"How would you like to feel?"

"I would like them to stop doing it."

"Is there anything we can do to stop it?"

"Yeah, we can go our separate ways. I ain't living with that."

"Is there no other solution?"

"Nope."

I tried to stimulate more discussion about thinking, self–talk and perception, what may be called *situation appraisal / reappraisal*. My goal was to encourage the man and the woman to locate their thoughts; but it wasn't going well. I chose to dig deep and use a technique where I would say a word, and the couple would just tell me what their immediate thought was in relation to that word. That way, I believed, they could be guided into hearing their own self–talk.

I used words like *home, love, church* and *meatloaf*.

"God, God, God, dinner."

We were getting nowhere.

I remembered how Al used the word *fuck* and how people responded to that word with such enthusiasm and variation. I asked, "How about the word *fuck*?

The man and his wife seemed unmoved. After a few seconds, however, the man said, "Mister, my thoughts is that if you say that ag'in, we'll be leavin'. Me and her don't talk like that."

"Great! What else do you say to yourself when you hear that word? What is your self-talk? Do you tell yourself that I am being disrespectful?"

The man paused before speaking.

"I don't think we think all that. We just think you shouldn't talk to us that way. That's about it."

I turned to the woman, "What about you? Do you find the word *fuck* offensive? Do you think I should stop saying it? Do you have any ideas?"

The woman recoiled.

"I done to'ed you, mister," the man said. He stood and ushered his wife to the door. "We thank you for your time. We wish you a fine day." The man took his wife's arm and walked toward the door. "I to'ed you we should just stay home," the man said. "Folks are just crazy. What'd he expect us to think?"

I learned that day, nestled snugly in the hills of eastern Kentucky, that the word *fuck* didn't elicit the same kind of response as it did for Al when I used it. I also learned that REBT is easy to practice badly.

✳ ✳ ✳ ✳

I grew and learned over the next few years, but I did not veer from the Al's theory and the idea of emotional intelligence that clearly stated that people make their own feelings by the way they think and perceive. I used the theory full-force with myself, but I was more reluctant to practice the theories too literally, with others. I kept in mind that *People are not disturbed by things; they are disturbed by their view of things.* I didn't hold back with my own emotional improvement, but I came to understand that if I were to continue to practice REBT and emotional intelligence theory with others, I would have to find my own style and leave Al's to Al.

* * * *

Working in eastern Kentucky presented me with many opportunities for building my REBT and emotional intelligence skills, not only as I practiced on myself, but with others. I learned that language was so very important to nearly everyone. So words and language were the keys to effectively communicating the principles of REBT and emotional intelligence theory. Without an awareness of how others hear words, interpret words and understand language, teaching the concepts would be an inescapable failure. I learned that it would be in no one's best interest for me to believe my that people understand without knowing, first, how they used words and language, themselves.

I first had to learn to *hear.*

* * * *

In addition to my job as a therapist, I was also tasked with investigating allegations of maltreatment of children. Our office regularly received anonymous calls from concerned citizens who, ostensibly, hoped to report occurrences of abuse and neglect they had either heard about, saw firsthand or simply imagined.

In truth, a majority of the callers were discontented with their neighbors for one reason or another and used our office to settle the score. In one particular case, the caller reported a mother of two who wasn't feeding them. "She *never* feeds them?" I asked.

"Nope," the caller said, "Never!"

When I arrived, I was met at the door by a rotund eight–year–old boy and his equally–well–fed four–year–old sister. I came inside the trailer and discussed the allegations of neglect with the children's mother. "Have a look around. See for yourself." She pointed toward the cupboards in her kitchen.

I found the cabinets well–stocked and a thirty pound turkey, frozen solid, sitting in the freezer. I reached up and took a can of soup off the shelf. "I like this soup," I said. "I buy it all the time." Upon picking it up, I realized immediately that the can was empty, staged to look as if the contents were still inside. The bottom of the can had been removed, the contents emptied and the can washed and placed back in the cabinet. I reached for a box of cereal, a can of beans, a can of ravioli. Each of the containers was empty. "I don't get it," I said, looking into an empty can of SpaghettiOs.

"Well," the mother said, flopping onto the kitchen chair, "we eat hot meals at the corner grocery twiced a day. They take our stamps down there. They cook better than I do."

"Why do you put these empty containers in your cabinet?"

"For people like you comin' around snoopin' and passin' judgment. *Makin'* me think I'm a *bad* momma and a *bad* person. Takes me a week to get over how bad you people *make me feel.*"

"Your children are eating," I said.

"That's for sure. It ain't worth all the hassle you people give me to just tell the truth. You *make* me so nervous; I need a pill every time you all show up."

Upon hearing that the woman believed that I was responsible for how she felt, and obviously didn't know it was her thinking and perception of me and what I represented that made her feel that way, I felt my REBT-therapist antennae rise up through the back of my head and I launched right into my role as a therapist. "What do you tell yourself when people like me come around? Do you tell yourself that if I think you are a *bad* mother that you truly are a *bad* mother? Do you tell yourself that my opinion of you outweighs your own opinion of yourself? Aren't we responsible for our own thoughts and emotions?"

The mother pulled her children close to her hips. "What in hell are you talkin' about?" The three of them looked at me as if I were speaking French. "'scuse my French," she added.

I took the woman aside. "If you think about it, you will realize that I don't *make* you feel. We *make* ourselves feel by what we tell ourselves about what we perceive." I put both hands on her shoulders and looked into her eyes. The woman stepped back. "You do *make* me feel. You *make* me feel bad about myself."

"I don't *make* you feel. That's magic. If I could *make* you feel, then I would *make* you happy and we would all go our merry ways. We *make* ourselves feel by the way we talk to ourselves. We have to change our perception and our self-talk."

"Are we done? You're scaring the kids."

"I guess you don't get it?"

"Yes I do get it! She said, slamming the cabinet doors. "It's another one of your tricks."

Giving up and walking toward the door, I stopped for one more question. "Hmmmmmm . . . so, anyway, why do you think someone would call social services and report you for not feeding your children?"

"They're jealous of my suit case." She pointed her finger at the wall, ostensibly at the neighbor to her left.

"Your suit case?"

"Yeah, I got a suit case down at the courthouse and they're just jealous of it."

"I'm sorry. I'm not following."

"I could get $5,000.00 from my neck. They're just jealous."

"Oh, you have a lawsuit."

"No, honey, I got a suit case. Now charge me or get out."

* * * *

It will be important to remember, as we progress toward improved emotional intelligence, that language plays such an important role in how we understand one another, and how we interpret the actions we take and observe other people taking, that the slightest change in inflection, twist of meaning or misunderstanding in pronunciation can present a number of unexpected emotional and behavioral challenges. I also learned that when people are in a state of stress, they are not only unlikely to hear, they are not likely to learn.

* * * *

We should never expect that anyone will immediately make the connection between their thoughts and their feelings, without first committing to a great deal more explanation than I was, so far, used to providing. I continued to remind myself of Al's final words to me: *It will take the force of will to do it.*

Chapter Two
Go Suck a Lemon

Visualize yourself standing in a grove of lemon trees, thick branches lined with thorns and smooth, green, shiny leaves. Hanging from the branches are clusters of perfectly shaped lemons, yellow ovals filled with seeds, juice and pulp. Focus your attention on the most wonderful lemon of them all, grouped among the smaller, less developed ones.

Standing beneath the tree, you reach your hand up and pluck the lemon from its place on the branch. As you pull it free, the limb snaps back and regains its original position.

You gaze at the lemon, sitting in the palm of your hand and you can feel its weight. Toss it in the air and let it land back in your palm. Roll your hand over its skin and feel its texture, the way it slides over your fingers. Raise the lemon to your nose and inhale its aroma, its scent, its freshness.

Breathe in *deeply*.

When you're finished examining the shape, texture and smell of the lemon, place it on a nearby rock. Take your pocketknife from your pants pocket and slice the lemon in half. Notice as the juice rolls out, puddles beneath it and runs down the contour of the rock.

Cut the lemon into wedges and arrange them in the shape of a star on the moss-covered rock. Choose one of the moist wedges and raise it to your mouth. Bite into the lemon and suck the juice and the seeds from it.

* * * *

The human brain is a remarkable organ, capable of extracting sensory information from thought, alone, allowing us to go well beyond the classical five senses, into another realm. This exercise depends on recall to replicate the sensory signals that simulate the actual corporeal event. Our potential for recalling tastes, odors, sensations and feelings lies within the strength of our imagination. We might recollect the taste of mint, bacon, Cheerios, a McDonald's cheeseburger, even water.

In very much the same way as we imagine taste, we can imagine emotion and feeling. For example, a convincing actor must recreate fear, anger, sadness and any number of other emotions found among humans simply by recalling their own experiences with those emotions.

Like an actor playing in a scene on stage, emotion can be recalled and replicated, as if the event were actually taking place in the moment. So, if we imagine we are being treated intolerably, we will think in those terms and our body will respond chemically to our thoughts and perceptions, sending stress hormones throughout our body to help us fight what we believe to be intolerable, unbearable or insufferable.

Our mind and body work together not only to simulate the taste of a real or imagined lemon, but also to protect us from the real or perceived threat we imagine. If we tell ourselves that we about to suck a lemon, our body will prepare us for that event. Likewise, if we believe we are being treated intolerably, and that we cannot stand it unless it stops, our body will prepare us to fight back or escape that event.

* * * *

In the same way the lemon causes us to salivate, simply by thinking about it, when we *think* we are being treated badly, stress hormones are released into our bloodstream and bring us to a hyper–aroused state, ready to fight, flee or freeze.

* * * *

Now imagine a bowl of brightly colored jellybeans; yellow, green, red. Let the colors and flavors flood your imagination. Which one will you choose? Dipping your fingers into the middle of the bowl, you feel their shiny surfaces pass over your fingernails. You study them, scanning the colors for flavors you don't care for and those you prefer.

You pop a few jellybeans into your mouth. The sugarcoated beads begin to melt, as your saliva washes over them. You bite into the hard shells and allow the sweet tastes to run together. Cherry, tangerine, lemon, green apple, grape and licorice wash over your tongue and down your throat.

A suggestion of cinnamon begins to invade your mouth, first by nipping at the tip and sides of your tongue, distorting the taste of the other jellybeans. Your tongue sizzles as the flavor starts to overwhelm your senses, searing your tongue and cheeks with a bite only red hot cinnamon can induce.

The flavor is inescapable. The red bean is seemingly toxic, mouth–burning, incapacitating to your taste buds. You chew quickly, the sugar granules grating your teeth like particles of sand.

* * * *

At a time in the distant past, humans depended on a nature–given, automatic response to help reconcile very real or potential menaces to life and limb. Nature allowed for the use of facts and the fictions of perception to maximize our response time to threat. We don't actually make an agreement with our bodies to respond to real or imagined hostility. Our stressful thoughts were sufficient to initiate that *fight-or-flight* response.

Much like our imagination can conjure the taste and sensation of sucking the juice from a lemon or crunching into a cinnamon jellybean, our perception of imagined danger, e.g., disrespect, insult and verbal injury initiates a sequence of hormonal and neurochemical events that depend on thought to activate the very same protective response.

In today's world, threats from bears and lions have been replaced by rude and unfriendly people, the culture of employment, money and family problems. Those kinds of hazards are ever–present in the lives of most people, resulting in what was once a life–saving response, intended to take seconds, now potentially lasting the length of a full day, a week and even years to dissipate.

The extended secretion of stress hormones introduced through potentially manageable thought can have an impact on the integrity of our major organs. Increased heart rate, blood pressure and respiration can result, among other things, in hypertension, obesity and heart disease. It appears that Nature's intention to protect mankind from harm using perception alone may now be inhibiting our survival.

＊＊＊＊

The fundamental use of emotion may be to help us avoid danger and maximize safety and reward. Our brain facilitates emotion often using perception (thinking) alone, regulating hormones, neurochemicals, the thalamus, the pituitary gland, body temperature, the adrenal glands and many other vital activities to accommodate accurate or faulty perception, equally.

＊＊＊＊

Let us imagine that the lemon, this time, is sitting in the refrigerator, cool and ready to be squeezed. We take the lemon from the refrigerator, feeling the coolness of its skin on your fingers. At the sink, we turn on the faucet and run water over the lemon, gently washing it with our fingers. The water beads up on the lemon's skin.

We place the lemon on a wooden cutting board and watch as the water from the kitchen faucet settles beneath it. We take a stainless steel knife and draw the sharp edge over the lemon, slicing it precisely through its middle. The juice seeps out and mixes with the water beneath each half. We see the lemon seeds sitting on the surface of the fruit. We raise one of the wedges to our mouth; bite into it and chew.

As we chew the lemon, the suggestion of cinnamon begins to invade our mouth. Our tongue sizzles as the flavor starts to overwhelm our senses, searing our tongue and cheeks with a bite only red hot cinnamon can induce.

The flavor of the cinnamon is inescapable. We take the lemon out of our mouth and study it. *Is this a lemon or a cinnamon jellybean? It sure looks like a lemon, but it tastes like a cinnamon jellybean.*

We return the wedge to our mouth. The red bean is seemingly toxic, mouth–burning, incapacitating to our taste buds.

* * * *

Exchanging the taste of the lemon with the taste of cinnamon is similar to exchanging one emotional response for another. Getting our old beliefs to taste less like lemons and more like jellybeans will present us with a number of sensory challenges.

It is tough to imagine two independent tastes simultaneously. For example, we can experience the same event where we believed we were treated intolerably and perceive it differently. We may imagine, instead, that we are being treated differently from how we had expected, but the treatment is far from intolerable. In fact, we can tolerate the treatment quite well, if we believe we can, thereby exchanging the taste of the lemon for the taste of cinnamon.

* * * *

It is likely that the human emotional system is still quite primitive. Social and physical threat initiates the same response system in the brain. To the brain, in many ways, a wild boar is as dangerous as an inconsiderate, disrespectful motorist. Only one, however, truly poses a genuine threat. The other is simply a product of imagination.

We may not yet have developed a pathway in our brain that allows for rational thought, when we perceive, rightly or wrongly, that we are being threatened by someone's words or behaviors. For example, if we are making ourselves angry, because we are thinking in a particular way, we are not likely to simply stop and express forgiveness or sadness without first stopping and making an effort to change our thinking.

* * * *

We are capable of immense emotional growth, but we may choose to remain unchanged, even in the face of contradictory information. Essentially, people do what they did last time if it worked. Drug addicts take drugs because it works. People shout at other people because it works. People depend on approval from others, because it works. Unless provoked, and in the absence of trauma, people will rely on automatic thought processing, rather than taking a moment to reconsider our thoughts and taste the jellybean.

* * * *

It is unlikely that we have an area of our brain dedicated to biting into a lemon and tasting cinnamon – or thinking angrily but, instead, expressing sadness and forgiveness. To accomplish that task, to improve emotional intelligence, we will have to build a working, mental model of how to achieve that goal. It will take the force of will to do that.

Chapter Three
Self-Talk

Our current level of emotional intelligence is a product of social emotional learning, a result of acquiring life skills, primarily skills in *cooperation, collaboration* (and, at some point, *copulation*) in a manner familiar and suitable to others within our particular social environment. Unfortunately, most social and emotional learning takes place within the confines of a single culture, a *tribe* if you will, making the acquisition of a broader set of social skills more difficult to attain, prior to adult independence and our eventual interactions with other tribes, other customs and behaviors and uses of language.

Like most of us, my own social-emotional education began at birth; and seemed to pick up steam in elementary school, where I learned that burping loudly in the lunchroom, eating chalk, throwing burrs onto woolen hats, clowning and teasing could set people ablaze with emotional color, merely by fine–tuning my skills at needling, nettling, nudging, peeving, perturbing, pestering, plaguing, provoking, riding, riling, teasing, ruffling feathers and, notably, pushing buttons!

"You really know how to *push my buttons*!"

"Stop doing that! You're *making* me nervous."

"You're a *bad* boy!"

At the doctor's office, for instance, I watched as children waited for their vaccinations – *bee stings*, as they were euphemistically called. To this day I cannot imagine why anyone would tell a child something *only* felt like a bee sting, to calm them before an injection. As if the similarity between an injection and a bee sting would somehow help reduce or even eliminate a child's anxiety.

Regardless, these bee stings seemed to have a unique, distinctive effect on each child who was about to receive one. Some children were stunned with fear, crying and pleading. Some bargained; some implored. Some played with toys, while others slept.

Ever on the lookout for evidence of my sister's weaknesses, I made a careful accounting of her fears. I was delighted to watch as she bolted upright, eyes bulging from her head, frozen with fear simply at the sound of her own name coming from the nurse's mouth. When it was my turn; however, I flailed, kicked and screamed, while my sister took careful mental note of my weaknesses. (I had my share of bee stings and I knew that only an idiot would stand still while one stung me.)

* * * *

The House of Horrors at Nantasket Beach was another time for me to observe emotion in other children. *Come on, it will be fun.* The clown's big, plastic left eye hung over its laughing rouged cheek, bobbing back and forth, keeping time with its pink, slick tongue. *I don' wanna.* I noticed very keenly how boys my same age went willingly inside, not even hesitating, grinning at me as they ran up the metal ramp and into the dark black hole that served as both the clown's mouth and the entrance to evil.

Why couldn't everyone go inside the *funhouse* and have as much fun as everyone else, welcoming this fear–filled event, enjoying the experience rather than being terrorized by it? What was the difference between us?

You're just a scaredy-cat.

* * * *

I particularly remember baseball. By no stretch of the imagination should I have ever been allowed to play any game involving running toward something fixed and a ball. I was so near–sighted I couldn't distinguish a ball that was heading for my face from one a mile above my head. Each time I took my turn at bat, already having convinced myself that I would never hit the ball anyway, I watched as the Killian brothers sat on the bench and, as if synchronized, put their arms over each other's shoulders and began to cry. My father watched it all from the sidelines.

* * * *

I was keenly aware, at this time in my adolescence, that failing at baseball, being afraid of the funhouse and my father's relentless disappointment meant I was a complete, overall, irredeemable failure as a male. I reminded myself of this every time I had to play baseball, swim, tell time or, generally, fail at anything. That same self-destructive thinking began appearing in other parts of my life, as I attempted and botched various challenges in my teen years. I grew into adulthood, but the nutty judgment I had fine-tuned since childhood continued to influence my appraisal of my human worth right into adulthood. I was a failure, even before I started.

* * * *

Emotional intelligence theory and REBT propose that emotion is the *language of the mind* – a language learned through exposure and repeated experience, shaped by thought and expressed through behavior.

Each of the social-emotional learning experiences I've described from my own life contributed, bit–by–bit to my knowledge of myself and how I would later in life encounter and manage the experiences I had in a broader culture.

Upon reaching my teenage years, I had assimilated to believing that:

* Fear is a weakness and should be denied, especially in males;

* Males behave differently than females. (Unlike females, behaving fairly, considerately, apologetically or gently was viewed as a serious, shameful oversight of my masculine accountability.);

* My grades, I learned, were a true and accurate reflection of my intelligence and, by default, my human worth;

* Athletic ability and sports interest, it turns out, were the only true measures of masculinity;

* Being popular among my peers was the only way to measure the value of friendship. If I wasn't popular, I wasn't valuable. I was a failure:

* Praise meant I was good;

* Disapproval meant I was bad;

* *If you are different, keep it a secret*; and,

* If anyone knows you're different, you will be scorned and disliked and you wouldn't be able to stand that.

That in mind, I learned to play a role and recite a script . . . to be perceived as *normal* and *good*. I could *never* fail. Or at least, no one could ever find out about it.

✳ ✳ ✳ ✳

Truth, the foundation from which I viewed myself and the others with whom I lived, had everything to do with how I was socialized, who was explaining truth to me and how I was growing, developing and learning to navigate the world using only those preset compass points.

I know now, in retrospect, that very little of the social emotional learning I was exposed to in my early life was helpful for adult-living. Later on, when all of that information was firmly wired into the neurons of my brain, I wandered away from my family of origin, consistently running into push-back from others not familiar with my tribal rules. I slowly began to realize I would have to find something *truer*, if I were to live the rest of my life sanely, with others.

✳ ✳ ✳ ✳

That weekend in Chicago with Al, I was introduced to the idea that social-emotional learning was a process of acquiring and assimilating to a set of *absolute* and *unconditional musts*, taught to us by our most trusted advisors, e.g., our mothers, fathers, grandparents, aunts uncles, close family friends; the rules we acquire through repeated experience within a particular environment.

By *absolute* and *unconditional*, Al meant that people are generally taught social-emotional thoughts and behaviors by their primary caregivers, within their family of origin. This kind of truth leaves little room for freedom, flexibility or personal judgment in how we think and perceive outside that environment. For example, if we are spanked, ridiculed and criticized by our family members when we don't behave according to the established truths, that same reaction to weakness and noncompliance can become the truth from which we will interact with others later on in our lives.

Most *absolute musts*, Al told us, were not only categorical, but *self-defeating*, likely to lead to unhealthy relationships with ourselves and others. "We believe we must encounter only events that unfold in a certain, familiar way. We tell ourselves that we cannot stand variation and we cannot be content unless things are the way we demand they should be," Al said. "If they are not, then we tell ourselves we cannot be content unless things change to suit us. We tell ourselves that others absolutely *should, ought, must, have to* and *need* to cooperate with our absolute demands or it's a goddamn shame and we can't stand it!"

Al asked everyone in the group, that weekend in Chicago, to list their most emotionally damaging absolute and unconditional musts. I came to refer to my own list of absolute, unconditional musts as my *Ten Essential Demands*:

* People must never disagree with me;

* To be content in life, I must be approved of by all people at all times;

* I must be involved in an intimate relationship to be lovable;

* I must be loved to be of any value;

* I must succeed to be viewed as good; if I fail, I must be bad;

* People must cooperate with me at all times under all conditions;

* People who refuse to cooperate with me must be ridiculed and damned;

* I must get what I want immediately and when I don't I can't stand it;

* I can't stand it when I cannot stand it; and, so, I must not stand what I cannot stand; and, finally,

* If it were true then, it must always be true.

Needless to say, after uncovering these insane *musts* in my thinking, these conditions I placed on my own contentment, these absolute, unconditional ideas I carried around about the world and my place in it, thoughts that influenced my ability to reason and to live contentedly among others, I set in my mind, immediately after leaving Chicago, to seek counseling!

* * * *

Conveniently, part of my clinical training in counseling required that I actually be a client seeking help from a therapist. In retrospect and considering my nutty frame of mind, I understand completely how this rule was arrived at.

My program's expectation for my *complete education* was that a better–informed therapist would be one who knew what it was like to sit in the client's seat, to have a real–life educational experience and to possibly achieve a higher level of personal insight and, as a result, build character.

I sought out a therapist to fulfill my 10–hour/10–session obligation to my graduate school, one who might also build on my emotional intelligence using Al's REBT theory. I began by registering with the student counseling center and getting a therapist assigned to me. "Do we have a preference?" the girl asked, seated comfortably behind the desk.

"A preference?"

"Oh, most folks have a preference for a male or a female therapist," the girl replied. "Do we have a preference?"

"Can *we* recommend one?"

"Not sure I'm allowed. I think they're all pretty much the same. Wouldn't want to *make* any of them mad by showing a preference." She winked and turned the pages of the appointment ledger. "Let me see who's available. Have a seat, please. We'll just go with the luck of the draw."

＊＊＊＊

The counseling center was as one might expect, a former Victorian style, single family home with a zillion painted–over fireplaces, retro–fitted cubby–spaces that nicely transformed the building into awkwardly meandering faculty cubes and therapy offices. Paint peeled from the ceiling and hung like stalactites. A faint, musty odor hung in the air. A bulky staircase covered in dusty, aged yellow shag carpet hulked behind the over–sized double front doors. Posters of kittens and rainbows were stapled to the waiting room walls, imprinted with slogans like *Even if happiness forgets us a little bit; never completely forget about happiness,* and, *The best way to cheer ourselves up is to try to cheer up someone else.* Of course, there was the old standby (the emergency poster) detailing how some ethereal being carried some guy across the beach and turned two sets of footprints into one. The coffee table was strewn with old *Cosmopolitan* magazines: *Is your Boyfriend Right for You? Find out in 5 minutes! Take the Test!* A box of Kleenex was set precisely beside each chair.

The therapist began by asking me how she could help me. Her body language was somewhat animated, spirited, as if she were preparing to open a surprise Christmas present on her lap.

"I'm not really sure," I said, "I have this class assignment to speak with a counselor for ten hours, so here I am. Not at the same time, though. Like over ten weeks." I handed her my assignment sheet.

"Oh, yes! How nice," she said, handing it back. I settled back in my chair. "We get these all the time. I'm a student too. I'm sure we can find something to discuss. Do you have anything in mind?"

I thought for a moment, literally placing my finger on my temple. I imagined telling her about my biases, my nutty beliefs and my experiences with Al that weekend in Chicago; but surely she already knew about Al. I thought I'd just cut to the chase. "Well, I don't like it that I am losing my hair. Is that worth talking about?"

She kept her eyes on me, while reaching for a nearby box of Kleenex, "That *issss* something," she said and cleared her throat, "How does that *make* you feel?"

"I feel like an old guy," I said, "like, I'm only 23, but I feel like I look 53."

"You look wonderful." The therapist leaned forward and grasped my hand, "You're a very handsome man . . . boy. Have you thought of wearing a cap?"

"Not really. I sweat a lot."

She lowered her voice to a whisper, "How about a nice hairpiece? I hear Hair Club for Men performs miracles."

"Yeah, but I'm 23."

She leaned forward, as if preparing to tell me I had twelve minutes to live. She looked around, then back at me and spoke even more softly. "We have a self–esteem problem. The first thing we have to do is get us to a place where we *don't care* what people think of our bald . . . lack of hair."

"Where is that place?"

"Well, silly, we have to make a list of all our positive qualities and focus more on those things than on our weaker qualities." She folded the pages of her legal pad to an empty page. She wrote the words GOOD and BAD at the top of her tablet and underlined them, twice. "Do you have any positive qualities?"

"I already feel pretty good about my positive qualities."

She peered at me over her glasses, troubled with my answer. "Sounds to me like we're pushing back."

"Goodness, really?"

"Yes! I will have to consult with my clinical supervisor. Do they let you do more than 10 sessions?"

* * * *

I remember sitting in the waiting room of the counseling center, eating my lunch, several weeks after my first session with the therapist, anticipating the start of my fifth or sixth session. I was reading a book on generalized anxiety, astonished at the uncanny similarities between myself and the diagnosis. Later in my education, I recognized myself in nearly any diagnosis I read about; schizophrenia, borderline personality, oppositional defiance, bi–polar and, of course, attention deficit hyperactivity disorder were all familiar to me. You name it; I had it. I listened to the two women sitting beside me, talking about their feelings. "So what's up now? I thought you were getting better," one of them asked.

"No, I'm still getting depressed again."

"Again?"

"Yeah," the other responded, evidently dejected and discontented.

"What happened to your therapist?"

"We broke up," she said, reaching for something in her purse. She offered her friend a mint. "He said I *made him feel* anxious."

"That's OK. You're cute. They'll assign you a new one." She accepted the mint and popped it into her mouth. "Do I have bad breath?" She blew into her palm.

"Yeah, I hope they assign me that new one, the young guy with the great hair." They both looked in my direction and smiled, simultaneously.

Just as Al had predicted, the saner I wanted to become, the less sanity, it seemed, I would be seeing in the people around me. I suddenly realized I was alone in my journey for improved emotional intelligence!

* * * *

That weekend in Chicago with Al, he talked a lot about how we use our *inner language*, our self-talk, with limited variability, to determine how we will feel, from the death of a loved one to lying, being ridiculed, being bald, stealing, being in love, getting a failing grade, cheating and social injustice. Al said, "If you want to improve your emotional intelligence, you will have to learn to speak a new emotional language!"

* * * *

My first day of high–school French was like being kicked in the throat with a Louis Vuitton.

"Bonjour classe!"

"Comment allez–vous aujourd'hui, madam?"

"D'accord. On y va!"

French was an indecipherable code; a landscape of rolling Rs, simply noise. My first reaction to the French language was to protect myself from it. To stay contentedly within my American English comfort zone.

I was taught through emersion, something like being dipped in French. I was expected to speak French all the time, even when I couldn't speak any French at all. When the odd occasion arose, and I was allowed to speak English, I was noticeably relieved, as if being released from confinement.

"Avez-vous des questions?" my French *professeur* would ask, after meeting with me concerning my failing grade.

"Non," I said.

"Voila! C'est finis!" she would say, placing her hands on the desk and standing, "On y va!"

I could feel the hand of the *Language of Love* reach over and cover my mouth. "But I'm not finished!"

"En Français," she would immediately say, "Maintenant, en Français."

"Ummmmmmm . . . J'ai besoin de plus de temps. J'ai beaucoup plus pour parler!"

"Très bon! Mais je n'ai plus le temps. Nous pouvons parler demain. OK?"

"D'accord . . . but I don't like it."

"En Français!"

"Non! Si vous plait! Je ne peux le faire plus!"

* * * *

For many of us, language brings comfort and provides safety. Language can be used to lash out at our enemies and to woo our lovers. Language can initiate war and negotiate peace. French, however, did not offer me comfort or safety at all. It provided confusion. I couldn't convey my emotions or express my thoughts or desires without frustration.

Prior to learning to speak French, I took language entirely for granted. Being forced to speak only French, I couldn't beg for a better grade, go to the boys' room, sharpen my pencil or explain my tardiness without first laboring through the rules of the French language.

French, I believed at the time, was a challenge not only to my intellectual development, but it also impacted my social and personal growth. Trying to maintain my status as a gloomy, sullen teenager, while speaking French, was out of the question. Speaking French meant making mistakes in front of my peers; being ridiculed. If that weren't enough, I was being graded on my willingness to stand and, through trial and error, systematically make a fool of myself in front of my classmates. All of this at a time when self–consciousness and insecurity was the central forces in my evolving development.

I made no attempt to use an accent or show any level of enthusiasm. I slouched and pronounced every consonant in exactly the same way it would be pronounced by a rebellious, English–speaking young man with a troubled future.

I decided to push against it.

* * * *

If you've ever tried to learn anything new at all, especially things that are intended to replace something you've been doing for a long, long time (like the language we speak); you know it takes time, dedication and a certain amount of devotion to practice.

Learning something new also takes a clear level of passion, something I intentionally removed from my French language education. I didn't want to learn to speak French. I was content speaking English. Everyone I knew spoke English (except for Jacque Cousteau, but at least he tried). I knew my way around English. It fit. And it didn't hurt every time I wanted to say something.

Acquiring a new way to speak inside our own heads, to change the way we talk to ourselves, can present many of the same challenges. The similarities between learning to speak a foreign language and learning to hear and change our own inner language, our own *self-talk* to something more rational and self-improving, will become clearer as we progress toward improving our emotional intelligence. Suffice it to say, we will meet the same language barriers I described above, when we try to change our inner language. We will be asked to replace our self-talk with something new; a new way of talking to ourselves about situations we've faced many, many times before. We will be asked to reassess, reappraise and reevaluate our customary self-talk.

* * * *

Our emotional language, our self–talk, ordains our emotional reaction to the events we experience. We regularly confuse our own absolute musts as laws, truths and facts that everyone should follow when, in reality, our absolute musts are our own preferences turned into the demands and needs we apply to others.

We are capable of expressing boundless emotion, nearly all of which is intentional and nearly all of it drawn from the language of our minds. There is nothing natural about fearing failure, for example. People fail, and they respond to failure from the perspective they hold about failing. Likewise, there is no evidence for feeling guilt when we make mistakes. If we craft our internal emotional language in such a way as to view mistake-making a tragic, catastrophic event, this self-destructive thinking will likely result in an equally self-destructive emotional response.

On the other hand, if we encourage ourselves to try new things and not to be overly concerned if we succeed or fail at them, we might begin to emote differently. Changing self-talk, our inner, emotional language, will likely result in changing our emotional response to nearly anything.

∗ ∗ ∗ ∗

When I started challenging my own inner language, I wanted to give up, to return to the inner language I already knew and accepted. I wasn't always as content as I could have been, but at least I knew my way around my old self–talk. And it didn't hurt every time I wanted to think or say something.

Just like giving up our native tongue, we will cling to our learned emotional language because we know it so well. We rely on our self–talk to help us encounter life. It is comfortable and we will hold on to our way of thinking until we are convinced that the benefit of changing it outweighs the benefit of maintaining it.

* * * *

Although my early education in life revealed a world filled to the brim with a wide assortment of nuts, fruitcakes and people who were bat–shit crazy, Albert Ellis taught me a more durable, lasting and life–enhancing way of cooperating and collaborating with others and with myself.

Al told me that if I truly wanted to improve my emotional intelligence, I had to actively change the way I communicated with myself about myself and my relationships with others. I had to tell myself something different, something more fact–based, something *truer*. I had to overcome years of self–defeating thinking by taking responsibility for the emotions I produced from my own thoughts. I had to defeat the idea that any amount of needling, nettling, nudging, peeving, perturbing, pestering, plaguing, provoking, riding, riling, ruffling feathers, teasing and button pushing could have a crushing impact on my emotional state. I had to realize that I am the principle architect of how I make myself feel because I am the architect of what I think. Most importantly, I had to accept reality for exactly what it is, even when reality is not pleasant; and I reminded myself that it would take the force of will to do that.

Chapter Four
Sandy's Case

Background: Sandy is a black, Hispanic, bi-lingual, unmarried 29– year–old, female, cashier. Sandy has no children. She lives alone. Sandy is attending therapy for the purposes of discovering her motivation to overeat. Sandy hopes to be married someday and have children. She worries that she will spend her life alone, because of her weight.

Single Session

Therapist: How can I help you?

Sandy: I hate being fat.

Therapist: How is being fat a problem for you?

Sandy: Nobody likes fat people. I am always afraid that someone will make fun of me in public.

Therapist: Is there anything else about being fat that you don't like?

Sandy: I hate pretending all the time that I am happy being fat.

Therapist: Anything else?

Sandy: I just hate having to lie all the time and pretend people don't notice how fat I am.

Therapist: OK . . . anything else?

Sandy: That's about it. I want to be different. I don't want to be this way.

Therapist: Any of these things more important to you than any other?

Sandy: I guess that everyone hates fat people.

Therapist: Wow! That's really terrible. How do you know that everyone hates fat people?

Sandy: Because I'm fat and I know. I live through it every day.

Therapist: Do I hate you?

Sandy: I don't know. Do you?

Therapist: No.

Sandy: How do I know that?

Therapist: You'll just have to take my word for it.

Sandy: I'm lost.

Therapist: Yes, let's re–focus. I'm wondering if people generally liked fat people, how you would feel about that.

Sandy: I would be a lot happier.

Therapist: Would you want to be fat then?

Sandy: Yes. I wouldn't have any problems then.

Therapist: Would everyone like you then?

Sandy: I guess not. Someone wouldn't like me for some other reason.

Therapist: I don't think you are talking about being fat at all.

Sandy: What are we talking about?

Therapist: Maybe we are talking about how well we accommodate not being liked.

Sandy: Maybe, but I can change myself if people don't like me for other reasons. I mean if people don't like what I'm wearing or what I'm driving, I can change it. I can't change being fat. At least it wouldn't be very easy to do. It would take a lot of something I don't have. I don't want to lose weight. I just want to be liked for who I am.

Therapist: So if I didn't like your shirt, you would change it?

Sandy: I wouldn't change it, but I wouldn't wear it here again.

Therapist: What would it mean if I didn't like your shirt?

Sandy: I guess it means you don't like me.

Therapist: What if I didn't like you?

Sandy: I would feel like I was bad.

Therapist: Simply because I didn't like your shirt?

Sandy: I guess.

Therapist: Again, I don't think you're talking about being fat at all.

Sandy: Goodness. What are we talking about now?

Therapist: We are talking about you and how much you dislike yourself for any reason anyone can hand to you. We can actually do something about that. Do we want to do something about that?

Sandy: I never really looked at it like that.

Therapist: What would it mean if someone told you they didn't like you because you were fat?

Sandy: It would mean I couldn't make them like me right away.

Therapist: And what would it mean to you not to be able to make someone like you right away?

Sandy: I guess I would feel . . . like . . . powerless. Like I would be really off balance until they saw past my fat and liked me.

Therapist: Is it true that if someone didn't like you because you are fat that you are entirely bad?

Sandy: To them I would be.

Therapist: That may be. Is it true that you are entirely bad because someone doesn't like your shirt? Your car? Your weight?

Sandy: Not really. I mean it isn't true unless I think it's true.

Therapist: How do you know it's not true?

Sandy: Because they might not like me, but I have some friends who like me and don't care that I'm fat.

Therapist: I thought you said everyone hates fat people.

Sandy: I guess I was exaggerating.

Therapist: It may not be such a good idea to exaggerate when we're in emotional turmoil.

Sandy: True.

Therapist: So what's so special about the person we are talking about? The one who doesn't like you?

Sandy: I guess I want everyone to like me.

Therapist: Is it your goal to have everyone like you?

Sandy: I guess.

Therapist: We may want to work on that goal. It will take the force of will to do that.

Chapter Five
The Rules of Engagement

Many of us have fallen into an emotional rut.

After years of living and learning, our emotional lives have become quite foreseeable, predictable, a knee-jerk reaction.

We simply do what we've always done.

If I am treated this way, I will act that way.

If I am treated that way, I will act this way.

In fact, the repetitive nature of doing the same thing with our thinking and emoting every day strengthens those connections in our brains and how we will respond the next time something similar happens. Our response to stimuli doesn't have to make sense or bring good results. There just has to have a familiar corollary to what we've done in the past.

Our emotional responses are frequently reinforced by those around us; quite frankly, people tend to respond to adversity and misfortune in much the same way, because they teach each other how to behave. We strengthen those lessons every day through repetition and observation.

There is, apparently, a language of emotion that we share not only within ourselves (our self-talk), but also between ourselves. We not only support and reinforce our own responses to emotional hardship, but we teach each other how to respond, and we strengthen each other through continuous reinforcement:

"I can't believe he said that to me."

"Me neither!"

"What would you have done?"

"I would have done exactly what you did."

"Now I don't feel so bad about having to do that."

"It was the only thing you could have done."

"I knew I was right."

* * * *

Improvement in emotional intelligence may be related to how we hear and process our own inner language and learn to rely more on rational reason in how we think and behave, rather than a process of replication of how we've behaved in the past, interpret what others tell us about what we experience and how we use that information to develop our cognitive and emotional range.

"Do you think it's OK to feel so depressed?"

"Of course! What happened to you was awful. I don't know how you can stand it."

"Yes, you're right, it is awful."

"Your feelings are very appropriate to the circumstances."

"Yes, I thought so too. How long do you think I should feel this way?"

"No telling. First, he will have to apologize and you'll have to heal and recover."

"I don't think he's going to apologize."

"Then I don't know what to tell you. Life is gonna suck."

* * * *

As a therapist who speaks nearly every day about the influence of self-talk on emotional health, I have come to some flexible conclusions. For instance, thinking about the worst of the past and the potential catastrophes of the future often leads to stress, anxiety and depression. There is, after all, no amount of worry that can alter the past or predict the future to a certainty, leaving us feeling helpless. Even if we think optimistically about the future or joyfully of the past, by contrast, we can cause ourselves to feel dissatisfied, as we may deem the present inferior to a future or past event. An optimally balanced time perspective is a potential route to an effective emotional life.

If our contentedness depends on changing our past, we will remain as unchanged as our past is fated to remain. We cannot change a zebra's stripes. We simply must accept that they exist. Of course we can imagine better, but we must acknowledge what is, before we can achieve what could be. We may, instead, understand our emotional problems *in the present*, here-and-now:

"My father was abusive when I was a child."

"Is your father still abusive toward you today?"

"No, I'm 43 years old. And he died six years ago."

"Is your father involved in your relationships?"

"I think about my father when I'm on dates."

"What do you say to yourself?"

"I say if he hadn't been abusive, I wouldn't be single. I would have more dates. I may even be married and have children."

"Does telling yourself that story about your past help you enjoy the dates you have, today?"

"Not really."

We can listen to how we talk to ourselves and question the rationality of our beliefs as they exist in our thinking, now.

"If we tell ourselves we cannot be content until we reconcile and understand our past, how likely is it that you will ever be content?"

"Probably never, using that kind of logic."

"Can you tell yourself that you can be content, in spite of your past and the unfortunate things you experienced? Can you accept your past?"

"It will be hard."

"Will it be as hard as living discontentedly for the rest of our life?"

* * * *

Identifying our use of the absolutes in our self-talk will go a long way to helping us identify the kind of self-talk that is in immediate need of revision. Without conscious awareness of the inherent inflexibility of our thoughts, our emotional options will be quite limited. Turning our inflexible demands into flexible options may result in more opportunity for change and, as a result, improved emotional intelligence.

Less demanding, more flexible beliefs can help by assisting us in achieving a more competent, rational method of processing our thoughts. We can work forcefully, persuasively and vigorously against our tendency to think irrationally, using a system of logical, pragmatic evaluation of self–talk.

* * * *

Our beliefs are habitually confused with facts. If we are convinced our beliefs are facts, we will behave as if they were. Words like *should* indicate that the statement is somehow a law and that it must be upheld by everyone with whom we come into contact. Removing the absolute demand from the statement (the should) and recognizing that people will behave any way they choose, even when we believe they shouldn't, will result in some lesser degree of discomfort when we don't get what we *prefer*, in place of what we *demand*. That new belief is only possible, however, if we have the skill to challenge the previous belief with a more skillful judgment of the facts.

Thinking and perceiving and feeling are all interrelated, joined to one another so inextricably that it is often quite difficult to tell them apart. Improved emotional intelligence will include the ability to identify these corollaries and challenge their rationality and their contribution to creating the self-defeating emotions you express.

＊＊＊＊

It may be that we are always relying on the past and the future to determine our emotional reactions to every-day events. Society teaches us very early in life the rules of engagement with others within a particular culture, helping us to predict the future using the past as a gauge. We learn to describe the source of our discontent in terms of how other *people make us feel* when they break our previously established rules of engagement. To begin the process of improving emotional intelligence, we might first consider reviewing our historical self-talk, identifying our use of absolute demands, and becoming aware that it is not the events we experience that make us feel. It is our view of the events.

＊＊＊＊

Previous to my weekend in Chicago with Al, no one had ever asked me to locate the source of my emotions. It certainly never occurred to me that my emotions were almost entirely a product of my own thinking. I was under the impression that my emotions were just there, like berries on a bush, fungus on a rock, sand on the beach. They weren't exactly physical things that could be located and described through science. My emotions came from my gut, from my heart, somewhere below my head. According to Al, my emotions were not in my stomach or in my neck. My emotions were in my head, in my thinking. My thoughts may be fleeting, or hard to pin down, but my emotions were connected to my thoughts, nonetheless.

* * * *

Beliefs guide our behaviors and can impact our physical and emotional health. Like a virus, beliefs can spread, bolstering the strength of our other beliefs. Like any virus, its potential for life depends on feeding it the right nutrients to keep it alive.

Challenging irrational, unhealthy self–talk is what is needed to attack the virus, swooping in to destroy the unhealthy belief, helping us regain emotional equilibrium and health. As a culture, we may share many of the same dogmatic, unalterable beliefs:

He should apologize!

She should thank you!

You must be respectful!

Although we may continue to have the same expectations of one another, within a particular social structure, to a large extent, our brain has been prewired to receive information related to social-emotional learning, how we recognize the social traditions within a particular group, as a way of ensuring the survival of our species.

Social rules were once the things that ensured that humans would pass on the most useful traditions for cooperation, collaboration and copulation as members of a unique society. It has been many, many centuries since these rules were so explicitly necessary that to defy them would threaten the survival of humankind. We still tell ourselves such things as:

* I should be treated with respect. If I am not, it is awful and I couldn't stand it. I must force that person to show me respect,

or I will be ridiculed and lose my place within the social structure.

* I need affection. If I don't get it, it is awful and I couldn't stand it. If I don't get affection, it will threaten my ability to reproduce and I will live alone and lonely.

* I must never be criticized. If I am, it is awful and I couldn't stand it. If I am criticized, I will appear weak and I can be taken advantage of by others in my group.

* I ought to never fail when I try my best. If I do, it is awful and I couldn't stand it. If I fail after trying my best, then I am weak and I will not be respected and I will lose my place within the group.

* I need to be valued by others. If I am not, it is awful and I couldn't stand it. If I am not valued, I will be devalued. If I am devalued, I will lose all privilege as a member of this group.

These beliefs are still widely held, although they are not nearly as necessary to hold as they may have once been 10,000 years ago. They have been, instead, rendered irrational and harmful through time.

Applied to our modern world, our primitive standards of behavior still bring emotional discomfort whenever the expectations implicit in them are not met. It is now possible to live more individually, less fearful of breaking a social rule and, thereby, forfeiting one's potential to procreate and flourish as a member of a small group or tribe. We are now capable of more rational thought in relation to how we interact with each other.

* I prefer to be treated with respect. If I am not, I can still live contentedly. I don't need anyone's cooperation to live contentedly.

* I enjoy affection. If I don't get it, I can still be a valued human being. I don't need anyone's cooperation to live contentedly.

* I appreciate not being criticized. If I am, I can stand it. I don't need anyone's cooperation to live contentedly.
* I like to succeed when I try my best; but it isn't a condition of my contentment. I don't need anyone's cooperation to live contentedly.

* I would rather be valued by others; but I can live contentedly when I'm not. I don't need anyone's cooperation to live contentedly.

These beliefs are not as widely held, but they are rational, not harmful and will likely bring emotional comfort, because the standards implicit in them are under the individual's control. We, as a species, in modern times are more likely to survive without the cooperation of others, so we can broaden our thinking to include our individual freedom for choosing our emotions, without threatening our place in the hierarchy of humankind.

* * * *

When we are asked to give up our inner language, our beliefs in ourselves and how the world should revolve around us, we are being asked to give up a well–established, time–honored belief. Giving up a belief is something like giving up a part of ourselves.

Many of our beliefs are warnings, personal messages, morals and ideas conveyed to us by someone we respected or something we experienced that proved important to us.

* Don't let anyone roll over you!

* Don't take anything from anyone.

* You are perfect. Don't let anyone tell you otherwise.

Think of one belief you hold that doesn't work especially well and give it up! How about your belief that people *should* under all circumstances, treat you well?

That is a belief ripe for the picking.

Sacrifice it!

If you're hesitating, join the club.

People can be counted on to hold on to and defend their beliefs until they have some other belief, something better with which to replace it. We cannot simply point out the errors in our thinking and expect to surrender them without a fight. We must first accept that our belief is harmful and then we must be willing to replace it with a new belief.

So let's replace our belief that we should be respected by all people at all times with a different belief related to respect. For example, I have very little power over how people choose to behave. People will treat me any way they choose. I don't have to like how people treat me, but I do have to accept that people possess the free will to choose their own behavior and I possess the free will to live contentedly, even when people make those choices. It's like trying to replace a bad habit with a good one.

* * * *

Everyone knows cigarette smoking is dangerous, but until a suitable alternative is developed to replace smoking cigarettes, something acceptable to that individual smoker, they will continue to smoke. The same goes for our crooked, irresponsible and irrational beliefs. Until we can replace our operational beliefs, the notions we use to make judgments, with suitable alternatives, those we're willing to accept, we will hold on to our harmful, irrational beliefs for the rest of our lives.

"Is it true that no one will ever love you again, now that your girlfriend dumped you?"

"Looks that way."

"If no one ever loves you again, what will that mean?"

"It would mean that my girlfriend was right about me. I deserve to be alone."

"If you were alone, what would that mean?"

"It would mean that I wasn't loveable."

"What does it mean to not be lovable?"

"It means I am not worthy of anyone's love."

"Do you really think that you are unworthy of anyone's love, simply because our girlfriend broke up with you?"

"Sort of."

"Were you lovable before you had our girlfriend?"

"Yeah, I had a girlfriend before this last one. She loved me, so I guess I was lovable."

"So, now that you got dumped by your girlfriend, you are entirely unloveable?"

"I see where you're going."

"Can you be loveable and be single?"

"I guess so."

"What do you have to do to change your feelings about being alone?"

"Change my belief about what it means to get dumped? Change the idea that I have to have a girlfriend to be loveable. Change my belief that to be viewed as lovable is so important that if I'm not viewed that way that I am useless and worthless."

"Yes, you could do that."

✴ ✴ ✴ ✴

It has been suggested that less demanding, more flexible beliefs can help improve emotional intelligence. The development of a belief may include any number of contributions from a large number of sources. A single belief can be composed of past experiences, your grandmother's hopes, world disasters and social customs we picked up and adopted as our own. If this is true and our beliefs are a collection of experiences, before we would be willing to give up a belief, we would have to weigh the consequences against the benefits.

It's as if I were offering $50,000.00 for a rusted '62 Plymouth Valiant. We would be intrigued, interested and highly motivated. We know we would be better off if we made the trade, but we would still want to know more. We might hold on to the car until we understood the offer more fully.

Are there any strings attached?

Are you trying to trick me?

Are you crazy?

People seem to instinctively hold on to what they already know, if to give up a belief means we will be left with a belief we don't accept. In the case of the '62 Plymouth Valiant, the concern may be a matter of overall well–being: *Will what I have to endure by selling this car outweigh the cost? Am I being hoodwinked? Is my car somehow more valuable than I thought? Will I be hurt by this deal?*

The surrendering of beliefs is reasoned in much the same way. The decision to give up what we already believe, what we depend upon to get through each day, includes issues of psychological safety, protection and wellbeing. Exchanging one belief for another seemingly exposes an individual to vulnerability. Even the slightest threat to one's physical and psychological safety can be perceived as a threat to the individual's very existence. So, to give up a belief, we will have to have a new belief, one we can trust and count on for safety, to replace the one we are forfeiting.

* * * *

Flexibility in our belief system may help us achieve a higher emotional competency. In addition, improved emotional intelligence can be cultivated if we work forcefully, persuasively and vigorously against our tendency to think irrationally and self-defeatingly.

"So you actually can live with being disrespected?"

"Sure I can. I wouldn't be at all happy about it, but I could live contentedly."

"But would you be angry?"

"Yes, but not as much."

"How would you reduce the anger you would feel?"

"I would change my belief. I would remind myself that people act against my wishes and I can still live and be content with my own life, when they do. Besides, I don't get to dictate to everyone how they should behave. People behave and, well, I just have to accept it."

"We can't do anything?"

"Well, I can. I can tell people how I would prefer they behave. But if I'm in a frame of mind where I have accepted that they have a choice to behave the way they choose, I will be in a better frame of mind when I am asking them to change. We don't listen when people are shouting and demanding things of us. Besides, I always have a right to ask for what I want. The hard part is remembering that I don't have any right to get what I want."

* * * *

Our daily lives are regularly filled with a number of challenges to our emotional state. In that frame of mind, it may seem impossible to exchange one irrational belief for a rational one. After all, when we are in conflict with ourselves or others, our rational mind is disengaged and it is unlikely that we will be considering a variety of emotional options. It will take the force of will to do that.

Chapter Six
$A + iB = C / D > E$

Emotional intelligence theory incorporates bio-psycho-social philosophies of emotional and physical wellness, in addition to emotive and behavioral measures to encourage the learner to independently act against irrational thoughts and behaviors. By expressing a more internally-locus-ed base of control, and staying well–focused during the process of problem identification and resolution, improvement in emotional intelligence is believed to be more likely.

The ABCs can be used to understand thoughts and emotions and to provide a method for taking action against thinking and perception that are producing undue stress and hardship.

(Remember, not all emotional problems rise to the occasion of using this model. There will likely be any number of inconveniences, setbacks and manageable disruptions in our day that simple time and patience will mediate and eliminate. Those issues we believe are unmanageable, problems that interfere with living a healthy emotional life, will be suitable for this level of evaluation and intervention. Of course we can use this model of problem-solving for any emotional issue we experience. Sometimes, however, shit happens and we just let time handle it.)

* * * *

The ABCs come from Albert Ellis' Rational Emotive Behavior Theory (REBT) and rely on the idea that human beings derive emotion from thought. Ellis' paradigm for emotional problem-solving provides us with a method for charting how we came to our unmanageable emotional consequence and how to transform our emotion to a more manageable emotional outcome. Ellis' ABCs give us a way of visualizing our thinking, thereby providing a method for overcoming our self-defeating thoughts and the emotions they produce, achieving an informed, evolved and more self-enhancing emotional consequence. The equation for solving emotional problems using Ellis' model is: $A + iB = C/D > E$ Where an (A)ctivating event plus an irrational (iB)elief equals an emotional (C)onsequence which can be divided into its working parts by (D)isputation to equal a greater (E)motional outcome.

The system is much easier than it looks and sounds. We will learn to use it, but first we will more clearly identify the ABCs and what they represent:

A: Activating Event
(iB) Belief
C: Emotional Consequence
D: Disputation
E: Emotional Evolution

We refer to the A as the activating event because it is the circumstance that instigated the thoughts and emotions we are experiencing. Simply said, something happened and it caught our attention and we want to manage a better emotional reaction to it. We might describe the activating event (A) in simple, verifiable terms.

Some examples of activating events (A) may be:

A: My boss criticized me.
A: The cashier was rude to me.
A: My husband doesn't love me.
A: I failed my test.

The iB is the beliefs we apply to the event (A) we are attempting to understand and manage. The iB will represent our self-talk. It is the iB (irrational belief) that we are most interested in discovering. iBs are those self-statements that include our absolute demands, our *absolute shoulds, oughts, musts, have tos and needs* that we place on ourselves and others. We will have to listen to what we tell ourselves about the activating event (A) in order to capture our self-talk and chart our beliefs (iB).

Some examples of beliefs (iB) may be:

(iB) People should never criticize me, or I will never be happy.

(iB) People should show me respect when they talk to me, or I will never
be happy.

(iB) I need respect to be happy in my life.

(iB) People must never make errors when judging me, or I will never be happy.

(iB) I have to have my husband's love to be lovable, or I will never be happy.

(iB) Waitresses must never behave badly when they serve me, or I will never be happy.

These are all fairly common beliefs (iB) that often lead to quite unfortunate emotional consequences.

Let's explore these two factors in understanding and improving our emotional problem-solving skills by charting an activating event from its origin to its conclusion.

(A)   My boss criticized me.

(iB)   My boss was harsh with me and he shouldn't have been. I need my boss to approve of me. My boss must always treat me with respect. I ought to be treated better than I am being treated, or I will never be happy.

(A)   The cashier is rude to me.

(iB)   Cashiers should always be friendly. Cashiers must be attentive to me. Cashiers ought to never make mistakes when they are serving customers. Cashiers need to be pleasant and helpful, or I will never be happy.

(A)   My husband criticized me.

(iB)   Husbands should never criticize their wives. I need my husband to show me respect all the time. My husband must never behave badly with me. My husband ought to please me at all times, no matter what he is experiencing, or I will never be happy.

(A)   I failed my test.

(iB)   I shouldn't fail tests. I need to pass all tests to be viewed as intelligent. I must be above–average intelligence to be

intelligent at all. I ought to pass all the tests I take because I studied, or I will never be happy.

Before proceeding, write out your own activating event (A) and the beliefs (iB) you have about the issues you are now or have experienced in your life, just for practice. Pay special attention to your self-talk and your use of the words absolute should, ought, must, have to and need to identify your beliefs.

The C in this paradigm represents the emotional consequence (the emotion we have as a result of experiencing the A and iB). The emotional consequence (C) may be described as sadness, anger, anxiety, depression, disgust, angst and worry.

We will contribute to our diagram by identifying the C:

(A)   My boss criticized me.

(iB)   My boss was harsh with me and he shouldn't have been. I need my boss to approve of me. My boss must always treat me with respect. I ought to be treated better than I am being treated.

(C)   I am angry, afraid and repulsed.

(A)   The cashier is rude to me.

(iB)   Cashiers should always be friendly. Cashiers must be attentive to me. Cashiers ought to never make mistakes when they are serving customers. Cashiers need to be pleasant and helpful.

(C)   I am outraged and angry.

(A)   My husband criticized me.

(iB)   Husbands should never criticize their wives. I need my husband
        to show me respect all the time. My husband must never
        behave badly toward me. My husband ought to care about me
        at all times, no matter what he is experiencing.

(C)   I am afraid and angry.

(A)   I failed my test.

(iB)   I shouldn't fail tests. I need to pass all tests to be viewed as
        intelligent. I must be above–average intelligence to be
        intelligent at all. I ought to pass all the tests I take because I
        studied.

(C)   I am depressed.

Before proceeding, add an emotional consequence (C) to the activating
event (A), beliefs (iB) we previously identified.

Remember, we will not have an emotional consequence (C) unless we
have a belief (iB) about the activating event (A). For example, if we
believe we should, at all times, be treated well by our boss, we are likely
to make ourselves angry when s/he doesn't treat us the way we tell
ourselves we need to be treated.

People do not become upset because something happens. People make themselves upset because they tell themselves something about what happened: A + iB = C.

* * * *

We've talked about the similarity between learning a foreign language and learning a new emotional language. When we speak to ourselves in terms of what *should, ought, must, has to* and *needs* to be for us to be content in our lives, we are imposing the inevitability of unmanageable, self–defeating and destructive emotional consequences on ourselves, because things don't always work out the way we demand they should. Our goal is to change our personal beliefs, demands and needs to more manageable wants and flexible and constructive preferences.

* * * *

Now that we've come this far using the ABCs, we may want to run out and start using them. It may be helpful to practice the ABCs until we can move the process through our mind, at will. There are still, however, the D (disputation) and E (emotional evolution) to learn.

The D in the ABC paradigm represents the essential process of disputing our irrational, self-defeating beliefs (iB). The D provides us with a method for identifying the irrationalities in our thinking and offers an opportunity to subject these irrationalities to a higher level of scrutiny. The D allows us to pinpoint our logic (or illogic) for maintaining our views. The D provides us with an opportunity for testing what we tell ourselves, for locating the rationale of continuing to think the way we do about ourselves and others. The D represents the active process of asking ourselves the right questions to get at the right answers to evolve our thoughts and emotions to something more manageable.

At D we will ask ourselves if our irrational beliefs (iB) are actually true (iB), or are they some ideal we are demanding that others hold. Do I really need cooperation from others to be content in my life? Can I live with it when people act against my wishes? Is it really so unbearable when I don't get what I expect? Is this something I want or something I think I need? Where is the evidence for this belief? Can I prove that this belief is true?

Disputing (D) our irrational beliefs (iB) is a learned technique that, like using the ABCs, is an acquired skill that takes practice. Disputation (D) provides an opportunity to make new judgments about unfamiliar and familiar dilemmas. By challenging our customary self–talk, our roles and scripts (iB), we can actually see how we create our own emotions (C) and, by disputing (D) the thoughts that lead to the emotional consequence (C), impede the generation of unhealthy, unproductive emotion.

Disputing (D) requires us to challenge our firmly–held beliefs. We might ask ourselves to provide evidence, a factual basis for our beliefs (iB). Ask ourselves to prove, for example, that people should be respectful of us (iB). Prove that our wife shouldn't divorce us (iB). Prove that our children should not forget our birthday (iB). The only possible evidence for any of these beliefs (iB) is that we don't like it or we would rather have it our way. That is hardly enough evidence to expect others to change their behavior.

Building our skill at disputing (D) will require that we become an expert in how we use the words absolute should, ought, must, have to and need and acknowledge the dangers implicit in using these words. These words give support to the notion that we are the guardian of truth, right and wrong, good and bad. These words represent our standard of excellence; our standards of perfection, the ideal behavior that we impose on ourselves and others. These words represent our limitations in improvement in our emotional intelligence.

Let's add the D to our running diagram:

(A)   My boss criticized me.

(iB)   My boss was harsh with me and he shouldn't have been. I need my boss to approve of me. My boss must always treat me with respect. I ought to be treated better than I am being treated.

(C)   I am angry, afraid and repulsed.

(D)   Is it true that I need my boss' respect to be content in my life? Where is the evidence that my boss must always treat me well? How have I come to believe that I should never be treated badly or disrespectfully? How have I determined that my boss' respect plays a role in my overall contentedness?

(A)   The cashier is rude to me.

(iB)   Cashiers should always be friendly. Cashiers must be attentive to me. Cashiers ought to never make mistakes when they are serving customers. Cashiers need to be pleasant and helpful.

(C)   I am outraged and angry.

(D)   Is it true that people must always be friendly to me? Is it true that I have to always be treated well to find contentedness in my own life? Is it true that when people behave against my belief that they are entirely bad and must be damned? Where is the proof for all this stuff I am telling myself?

(A)   My husband criticized me.

(iB)   Husbands should never criticize their wives. I need my husband to show me respect all the time. My husband must never behave badly with me. My husband ought to please me at all times, no matter what he is experiencing.

(C)   I am afraid and angry.

(D)   Where is the evidence that my husband must always behave the way I demand? Is it true that even when I behave badly that my husband must always treat me nicely? Where is the evidence that my husband must always be perfect to be married to me?

(A)   I failed my test.

(iB)   I shouldn't fail tests. I need to pass all tests to be viewed as intelligent. I must be above–average intelligence to be

intelligent at all. I ought to pass all the tests I take because I studied.

(C)   I am depressed.

(D)   How have I determined that failing is a clear sign that I am entirely a failure? Is it true that if I am not good at everything I do that I am not good? Is it true that when I fail I should be damned? Is it true that I should always succeed at everything I do?

The D helps us challenge the veracity of our beliefs and to hold them to a rational standard. We may find that we have quite a few more beliefs (iB) and a lot more disputing (D) to do before we fully understand what we are telling ourselves. Feel free to explore this possibility. Spend time with this diagram. It will become the source of improvement in our emotional intelligence.

Before proceeding, add a disputation (D) or two to the activating event (A), beliefs (iB) and emotional consequence (C) for the previously identified problem.

* * * *

Improving our emotional intelligence depends on our ability to turn anger into a variety of other, less unmanageable emotions such as sadness, frustration, tolerance, hopefulness or forgiveness. We can evolve to any number of emotional reactions that are more suitable for contentedness, simply by disputing (D) and evolving our thinking (E).

The E in the ABC paradigm is simply the end result of using the ABCs to manage our emotional consequences. The E represents everyone's ability to have an emotional evolution, to change, through more rational thinking, the emotional response we have to nearly anything simply by challenging our self-talk. If we were successful at disputing (D) our irrational thoughts at iB, we will likely be capable of exchanging our emotional response (C) for something less burdensome (E). The E represents our improved, more manageable emotional response!

(A)   My boss criticized me.

(iB)   My boss was harsh with me and he shouldn't have been. I need my boss to approve of me. My boss must always treat me with respect. I ought to be treated better than I am being treated.

(C)   I am angry, afraid and repulsed.

(D)   Is it true that I need my boss' respect to be content in my life? Where is the evidence that my boss must always treat me well? How have I come to believe that I should never be treated badly or disrespectfully? How have I determined that my boss' respect plays a role in my overall contentedness?

(E)   None of what I am telling myself is true. It is true that I can live contentedly in my life, even if my boss chooses to behave badly. I can get a new job. I can tell him what I think and what I would like. I have many options available to me. That in mind, I believe I am no longer afraid or repulsed. I am sad that my boss doesn't have the skill to communicate in a friendlier way. He is apparently emotionally handicapped, and I can accommodate that weakness in him. I was feeling anger, but now I am feeling less anger. I am also flirting with the idea that I can feel forgiveness for him. He seems like he is a sad person.

(A) The cashier is rude to me.

(iB) Cashiers should always be friendly. Cashiers must be attentive to me. Cashiers ought to never make mistakes when they are checking out customers. Cashiers need to be pleasant and helpful.

(C) I am outraged and angry.

(D) Is it true that people must always be friendly to me? Is it true that I have to always be treated well to find contentedness in my own life? Is it true that when people behave against my belief that they are entirely bad and must be damned? Where is the proof for all this stuff I am telling myself?

(E) It is not true that everyone must be friendly to me at all times. People can actually do as they please. I can live with how people behave and I don't have to think that it is the end of the world simply because people are rude. I can be sad and discontented that people choose to behave this way. I don't have to be angry. I can live peacefully even though people act poorly and against my expectations of them. I am no longer angry. I am sad that people choose to behave poorly toward one another. I was feeling anger, but now that I think of it, the cashier doesn't really have any real control over how I value myself. I'm not really angry anymore. I guess I'm just content that I am me and I'm not her.

(A)   My husband criticized me.

(iB)   Husbands should never criticize their wives. I need my husband to show me respect all the time. My husband must never behave badly with me. My husband ought to please me at all times, no matter what he is experiencing.

(C)   I am afraid and angry.

(D)   Where is the evidence that my husband must always behave the way I demand? Is it true that even when I behave badly that my husband must always treat me nicely? Where is the evidence that my husband must always be perfect to be married to me?

(E)   If I am going to stay married, it may be a better idea to understand that my husband is imperfect and makes mistakes. I make mistakes too. If we are going to be content in our lives together, we will both benefit from remembering that we are both imperfect. I can be more forgiving of his imperfectness and he may be more forgiving of mine. I am not longer afraid. I am forgiving. I was feeling anger, but now I feel forgiveness. He is my husband and he is flawed. I can live with that, and I can tell him what I want. I just can't expect to get it sometimes.

(A)   I failed my test.

(iB)   I shouldn't fail tests. I need to pass all tests to be viewed as intelligent. I must be above–average intelligence to be

intelligent at all. I ought to pass all the tests I take because I studied.

(C)   I am depressed.

(D)   How have I determined that failing is a clear sign that I am entirely a failure? Is it true that if I am not good at everything I do, I am not good? Is it true that when I fail I should be damned? Is it true that I should always succeed at everything I do?

(E)   If I fail a test, that does not mean I am a failure. I succeed at a number of things that would defy that logic. It really means I failed the test. I can study harder next time. I can ask for extra help. I can resolve that I am not very talented in this area. I don't have to be talented in everything I attempt. I can be content in my life if I fail. It would be more fun if I succeeded. But people do fail and I am probably likely to fail at something again in the future. It doesn't help for me to berate myself every time I do that. I think I can be more realistic about what failure means. I am no longer afraid. I am motivated! I was depressed, but now that I have a better sense of what I'm telling myself, I am glad for the opportunity to not succeed. I can live contentedly with myself when I fail. I can only do my best at getting better grades and studying. Maybe I can look for help from those who passed, so I will do better on my tests next time.

* * * *

We should keep in mind that a complete evolution of our emotional state is not always possible. For example, a reduction in anger is best understood by gauging it on a scale from 1-10. When we designate our feeling at (C) we may write Anger x 8. If our attempt at managing our anger begins at eight, but is reduced to a five after examining it using this diagram, we may view that reduction as an indication of success. It is also quite possible to go from anger to sadness, anger to forgiveness, anger to less anger.

The emotional evolution (E) will depend on how well we use our disputation (D) to make rational sense of our self-talk (iB).

Our potential to create our own emotional consequence through better, more rational self-talk is the gold standard for improving our emotional intelligence. This skill will come as we build our talents at identifying and confronting our irrational beliefs (iB) and replacing them with rational ones (D).

Now add an emotional evolution (E) to our disputation (D), emotional consequence (C), activating event (A) and belief (iB) for the problem we previously identified.

* * * *

I remember a student in one of my lectures.

"I don't get it," she said.

"Well, let's say we tell ourselves we need to have $5.00 in our pocket every day before leaving the house. Let's say we tell ourselves not only that we need the money in our pocket, but we have to, we must have $5.00 in our pocket every day when we leave the house. How will we make ourselves feel if we get to work and find that we've forgotten our needed $5.00?"

"I guess I would feel anxious and afraid."

"Let's say we tell ourselves that we would like to have $5.00 in our pocket every day when we leave the house. Let's say we tell ourselves we would prefer to have $5.00. We tell ourselves that we hope to have $5.00. What do we make ourselves feel when we get to work and we find that we don't have $5.00 in our pocket?"

"Would we rather be anxious and afraid or let down?"

"Let down?"

"So we changed our emotion through thinking, by changing one word in our self-talk! Tell me how that happened."

"Well, if I tell myself things must be a certain way in order for me to be content in my life, when they're not, I will make myself depressed, anxious, fearful and angry. If I tell myself I would like things to be a certain way, if I would prefer them or hope for that outcome, and it doesn't happen, I can be sad or something like that, nothing near as bad as angry and anxious."

"Yes, and by simply making our self-talk more rational and reasonable."

Our thoughts are the birthplace of our emotions. Beliefs that are self–defeating tend not to stand up to scrutiny. Self– defeating thoughts ignore the positive, exaggerate the negative, distort reality and over–generalize. Pay close attention to how we apply the words *should,* *ought, must, have to* and *need* in our daily life. These words are demanding of a perfect and ideal standard. We might not be best served by expecting the perfect and ideal behavior from anyone – including ourselves. If we get what we want, be thankful for it. It will take the force of will to do that.

Chapter Seven
Buttons Bells Triggers and Chains

I started my career as a New–England–born therapist in eastern Kentucky. My accent made me a local curiosity, much like a Martian – or sasquatch would have been viewed. Whenever I opened my mouth and my accent was detected, I immediately became dubious, a dangerous outsider. A Yankee!

The particular area of Massachusetts from which I come didn't help to deflect that stereotype. I pronounce many of my words with a somewhat British flair. For example, half is pronounced (haAHf); path (paAHth), bath (baAHth), can't (caHHn't) and, the old stand–by car is pronounced (CaAHH). One afternoon, I was working with a very discontented woman, discussing her continuing, unpleasant relationship with her boyfriend. "He makes me so mad," she said. "I wish I wasn't so mad, but I can't help the way he makes me feel." It seems she was so overwrought on this particular day with how her boyfriend was making her feel, she wanted to spend some extra time with me, discussing it in more detail.

My policy was to spend forty–five minutes in actual therapy and fifteen minutes talking about what the client had heard during the session. "I'm going to have to stay a few more minutes. I'm a mess," the woman said with a sigh.

"You caHHn't," I said, "I have another client. You know our agreement."

The woman drew back in horror.

"Is something wrong?"

"I don't know what they do where you come from, but we don't talk to folks like that around here."

"I'm confused?"

"You been doing that since I met you. I'm sick of it. You Yankees are just plain mean."

"What!? I didn't say anything. I said 'you caHHn't.'"

"See! You said it again!"

"CaHHn't?"

"I've had it. You really know how to push my buttons!"

"Buttons?"

* * * *

It is not uncommon to hear someone say, "He really knows how to push my buttons," or "I'm just yanking your chain." The implication being that we actually have buttons, chains and triggers and they are there for others to push, pull and yank at will. It doesn't matter how evolved, patient or emotionally mature we may consider ourselves This *imaginative idea* of having buttons, chains and triggers may inhibit or even prohibit improvement in our emotional intelligence.

So what are those damned buttons anyway?

Our buttons are illusory, magical descriptions of volatile, angry, fearful reactive places in our minds. For example, refusing to acknowledge the absolute right each of us has to behave badly invigorates those areas of our brain and turns on the stress response, instigating the urge to retaliate. Once this process is set in motion, we imagine that our button has been pushed, our chain has been yanked or our trigger has been pulled.

It will take courage and self-awareness to conclude that that we have no buttons and that our thoughts, perceptions and appraisals are responsible for our emotions – not buttons. Even though we might set our minds to focusing more on improving our perception and less on our imaginary buttons, chains and triggers, that wisdom won't keep people from trying to push, pull and yank them. We may prepare in advance for that eventuality:

* Breathe

Deep breathing stimulates the vagus nerve, releasing an array of anti-stress enzymes and hormones such as acetylcholine, prolactin, vasopressin, and oxytocin. Deep breathing notifies the heart, lungs, upper digestive tract and other organs of the chest and abdomen that we are safe and not under attack. The stress hormones in our bloodstreams, set off by thinking catastrophically will begin to dissipate and allow for the cortex to contribute to resolving the problem.

* Look within

Our thoughts and our perceptions are our own and, when we are being criticized, offended or insulted, we may take a look at the thoughts we are creating. I am not suggesting that we will ever like to be ridiculed, but we can stand it and we can still live contentedly when people choose to behave this way. As we confront our self-defeating thoughts, establishing newer, more self-improving thoughts, we will be improving our emotional intelligence.

* Practice Contentment

Make a conscious decision about the emotional person we want to be. We have the cognitive power to be content under most circumstances, but it will take practice and a heightened awareness of the irrational and rational thoughts we feed ourselves. We may practice detaching from ego-based thoughts and strive to connect to a vision of our higher self.

If we persist in thinking we have buttons, the least we can do is take responsibility for pushing them ourselves. To do that, we must first review our absolute musts, the demands we place on others and how we should be treated. We must then turn these absolute musts into preferences, desires and wants, building a newer, emotionally intelligent inner language.

* * * *

Once upon a time, there was a man on an elevator. It seems the man, facing a packed lift, entered, turned his back to the other passengers and innocently watched as the floor numbers rolled past, overhead. As the man stood, waiting to arrive at his floor, he felt a sharp object stabbing into his shoulder blade. He grumbled and moved a bit to the right to escape the jabbing object. "This guy really knows how to push my buttons," he thought. The object found its way under his shoulder blade, and the man grew angrier, placing himself off balance, pumping adrenaline into his bloodstream, preparing him for hostility: "People are so inconsiderate," he thought. "People should be more considerate. Inconsiderate people really know how to push my buttons!"

As the elevator approached his floor, he told himself that when the elevator door opened he would turn and give the perpetrator a piece of his mind. "How dare he stick his umbrella in my back?! The bastard is really pushing my buttons and he's going to get a piece of my mind, for sure."

The door opened to the man's floor and he was about to step out, but he was determined to address what he thought was the injustice of the man behind him, poking him with his umbrella. Preparing his words, he turned and stood face–to–face with a blind woman, holding a cardboard box, a ruler protruding from its corner. In an instant, the man's feelings of anger turned to guilt, "Hmmmm . . . have a nice day," he heard himself say. He hung his head and backed out of the elevator.

The man's emotions were a product of his thinking and imagination. There was nothing factual or true about what he was telling himself to make himself angry. The minute he changed his thoughts, however, he also changed his emotional reaction to the very same event. He had no buttons, of course; and he could have begun his thinking from a framework of patience and forgiveness.

* * * *

Skill for changing how we perceive, appraise and think about the events in our lives can be used in any number of other circumstances, from being treated disrespectfully, to grief, to rejection. We simply have to change how we perceive, appraise and think about a situation and apply different *meaning* to it.

* * * *

If the condition for our contentedness is based on how others behave, we are likely to be discontented quite often. People are liable to do just about anything, without any notice at all. We can evolve our emotion from anger to other more manageable emotions by thinking and perceiving differently. And we can be content, even when people make emotional and behavioral choices that are contrary to our own. To begin to improve our emotional intelligence, we will have to *own* our emotions, know that they come from us and our own thinking, rather than placing their origin on others.

* * * *

There is an element of selfishness in considering only our own perspective in any disagreement. Recognizing and accepting that people have a perfect, inalienable right to choose to act foolishly and irresponsibly will go a long way to improving emotional intelligence.

All day long, people make poor emotional and behavioral choices. Remember, laws don't prevent foolishness; laws establish the consequences of breaking the law. We have a right to make foolish decisions, and we exercise that right from time to time. Not to recognize that others have a perfect right to make poor choices is, well, selfish.

We make ourselves angry by perceiving selfishly, interpreting selfishly and emoting selfishly. It is quite selfish to demand that people act not according their own standard but, instead, our ideal standard.

Take a fuller perspective of the experience.

Apply a different meaning to the event.

Consider your own human potential for making poor choices. Try applying the consequences you hope when you make a poor choice. You've been thinking and behaving the same way for most of your life. We are inclined to place people and things that do not fit our ideal standard into a category of bad, simply because their choice didn't meet with our approval. We always have more than one option available to us for how we can respond to the choices people make.

* * * *

We will be more likely to improve our emotional intelligence the moment we realize that we have no buttons, bells, chains or whistles. We can learn to think twice, to review our first thought and, if we find that it isn't our most beneficial alternative, seek other, more satisfying substitutes. There are multiple emotional options available to us if we practice more efficient and fact-based thinking. It will take the force of will to do that.

Chapter Eight
Elliot's Case

Background: Elliot is a white, English–speaking, unmarried 17– year–
old high school student. Elliot is an only child. He lives with his father
who is an US Air Force chief master sergeant, and his stepmother, who
works at the Base Exchange. Elliot is attending therapy at the request
of his stepmother. Elliot recently told his father that he is gay, and his
father responded by shouting at him, slapping him in the face and
telling him he was no longer his son. Elliot's father also told him he
was filthy, an abomination, disgusting, a drug addict, a sex fiend and a

pedophile. He ordered him out of the house and forbade his wife to ever speak with him again. Elliot went to his room and his father left the home. His father has been away from home for three days. His stepmother worries the family is collapsing.

Session One

Therapist: How can I help you?

Elliot: I told my father I was gay and he slapped me and disowned me.

Therapist: How is that a problem for you?

Elliot: How is it a problem? What do you mean, how is it a problem for me? Jesus, how would it be a problem for anyone?

Therapist: I mean just that. How is your father's rejection of you a problem for you?

Elliot: I wasn't expecting that question.

Therapist: Then we are off to a good start. How is it a problem for you?

Elliot: I guess it's a problem for me because I want him to accept me.

Therapist: What does it mean when your father doesn't accept you?

Elliot: This is getting even more confusing.

Therapist: If your father doesn't care for you, what does it mean?

Elliot: It means he doesn't love me.

Therapist: Does it mean anything else?

Elliot: It means he doesn't respect me.

Therapist: Anything else?

Elliot: It means I don't live up to his expectations of me.

Therapist: Anything else?

Elliot: I think that's about it.

Therapist: Let's arrange all this information. You told your father you were gay and he rejected you. You took that to mean he doesn't love you; he doesn't respect you and you are not living up to his expectations. Is that correct?

Elliot: Yes. That's about the size of it.

Therapist: That is what you think.

Elliot: Yes, that is what I think.

Therapist: What are you feeling?

Elliot: I'm pissed. I'm angry.

Therapist: Sometimes when you are feeling anger, you are also feeling fear. What are you afraid of?

Elliot: I'm afraid my father thinks I am a piece of shit.

Therapist: Yes, I can see that. What would it mean if he did?

Elliot: What would it mean? It would mean that I am a piece of shit.

Therapist: Can it mean anything else?

Elliot: No.

Therapist: Your father's opinion seems to have the power to turn you into a piece of shit. Yes, I can understand your fear. You don't look like a piece of shit, but I'll take your word for it.

Session Two

Elliot: You're making fun of me.

Therapist: Of course not. But what would it mean if I were?

Elliot: It would mean you don't take me seriously.

Therapist: Of course I do. But what would it mean if I didn't.

Elliot: This is getting like exercise.

Therapist: It is like exercise. It's exercising our mind. Play along. What would it mean if I were not taking you seriously, aside from the waste of my time and your money?

Elliot: I guess it would mean that you think I'm a clown.

Therapist: What if I did think that? What would that mean?

Elliot: I suppose it would mean that I am a joke.

Therapist: You give me a great deal of power.

Elliot: How so?

Therapist: If I decide to not take you seriously, that would make you into a clown?

Elliot: I never thought of it that way. I'm not sure I want to agree with you now that you put it that way.

Therapist: You don't look like a clown, but I can take your word for it.

Elliot: I'm not a clown.

Therapist: OK, you are not a clown, but you are a piece of shit?

Elliot: I guess.

Session Three

Therapist: So, you are not a clown, but you are a piece of shit?

Elliot: I don't want to be either.

Therapist: What are you going to do, then?

Elliot: Isn't that your job?

Therapist: I'm not sure. What do you think my job is?

Elliot: To fix me. To tell me what to think.

Therapist: You seem to be doing fine telling ourselves what to think.

Elliot: I think I'm dizzy.

Therapist: Let's get back to your father. He doesn't like you to be gay. He has disowned you and shown you disrespect. You believe these events have turned you into a piece of shit. Is that where we are?

Elliot: Yes, I guess.

Therapist: What does a piece of shit feel like?

Elliot: Oh boy. A piece of shit feels like really depressed and really sad and really scared.

Therapist: That doesn't sound at all like how I imagined a piece of shit to feel.

Elliot: I'm not really a piece of shit. It is a figure of speech.

Therapist: Oh, that makes things easier. I was thinking I was going to have to call a plumber.

Elliot: Very funny.

Therapist: So what we really have with us today is **Elliot**, a 17–year–old male who is homosexual and who has been rejected by his father and now feels depressed, sad and scared?

Elliot: That about sums it up.

Therapist: Now we're talking.

Session Four

Elliot: I wish I didn't have to be gay. It would make things a lot easier.

Therapist: What about being gay concerns you?

Elliot: Everything.

Therapist: Goodness, what motivates you? I mean, if things would have been a lot easier, what compelled you to tell your father you were gay?

Elliot: I wanted to be honest with him and I wanted him to accept me.

Therapist: What did you imagine being honest and seeking acceptance would bring?

Elliot: Probably exactly what I got.

Therapist: Then why do it?

Elliot: I think it's best to be honest.

Therapist: And accepted?

Elliot: Yes, most of all acceptance. People need acceptance.

Therapist: Do they?

Elliot: Of course they do.

Therapist: What would it mean if people didn't accept us?

Elliot: It means that I am not acceptable, that there is something wrong with me.

Therapist: All that from someone not accepting you?

Elliot: Pretty much.

Therapist: Let me get all this straight. Your father rejects us, and we are a piece of shit? Someone doesn't accept you, and you are unacceptable? That is a lot of power to give to other people. It seems whenever someone thinks something about you, you immediately believe it's true. It's like someone put a spell on you and you become whatever they want you to be. You cannot have contentedness in your life unless everyone you meet loves and accepts you?

Elliot: Yes, I suck and you are just telling me how much.

Therapist: So I have that same kind of control over you?

Elliot: Obviously.

Session Five

Therapist: It must be tough having to go back and forth between being a piece of shit and being unacceptable. What do you suppose we can do about that?

Elliot: You can make me straight.

Therapist: How do you suppose that would help?

Elliot: People would like me.

Therapist: Goodness, is that all it takes?

Elliot: Yes. If I were straight, I wouldn't have these particular problems.

Therapist: Do you think all of your problems would be solved?

Elliot: Not all of them, but most of them.

Therapist: What about the problems you still have?

Elliot: I could work on those.

Therapist: You would still have problems?

Elliot: Yes, but not these problems.

Therapist: Being straight wouldn't solve all your problems?

Elliot: No, I would just have different problems.

Therapist: How do you suppose we can help you get to the point where you didn't have any problems?

Elliot: I would have to be perfect.

Therapist: If that's the only way we can be content with ourselves, shall we set that as our goal? To be perfect?

Elliot: Not really. I don't think I will ever be perfect. No one's perfect.

Therapist: How do you know that?

Elliot: The odds are you will have some problems or that someone won't like us for some reason that isn't under our control. That's just the way things are. No one's perfect. Straight people don't have the same problems as gay people, though.

Therapist: What kind of problems do straight people have?

Elliot: They don't have to worry about being ridiculed, taunted, rejected and laughed at all the time. People wouldn't be pushing my buttons all the time.

Therapist: Really? What about a straight person who is obese? How about a straight person who is covered in planters warts? How about a straight person with two heads?

Elliot: That's an extreme example, but I hear what you're saying.

Therapist: I don't think it's a matter of being straight or gay. I think it's what you think about being gay and what you are telling yourself about yourself. When we think about being ridiculed, what are we telling ourselves?

Elliot: When my dad ridiculed me, I thought, 'You don't care about me and I can't stand that.'

Therapist: Anything else?

Elliot: It's funny, but it was like I was looking for him to forgive me for being gay. I said I was looking for acceptance, but I was really looking for forgiveness. I was sort of saying, 'I know this is bad and that I am not perfect, but I want you to forgive me for turning out this way.'

Session Six

Therapist: What do you tell yourself about being gay? I mean, if someone said, '**Elliot**, you are a big faggot,' what would you tell youself?

Elliot: I don't know.

Therapist: Close your eyes and pay attention to your thoughts. Listen to your self–talk. What are you saying to yourself about that statement?

Elliot: I don't like it. That's for sure.

Therapist: What about it don't you like?

Elliot: My God, where do I begin?

Therapist: Listen for words like absolute should, ought, must, have to and need. Look for self–talk that contains those words. Just say whatever comes to your mind.

Elliot: People shouldn't talk to me that way. People should be more courteous. I should be less obvious and not appear to be gay. I should learn to act straight. I thought I had, but I must not be doing a good job. If I act gay, I am a piece of shit. If I act straight I am good. It's my fault that people are making fun of me. Acting gay is bad. If people know I'm gay that means I am not like other people and that is really bad. If someone calls me a faggot, I will have to stand up for myself and fight them. I really don't want to fight people. But if I don't fight them, that makes me a faggot. I don't want to be a faggot or fight. So I am just standing there. I'm not fighting and I am not running. But I look like a coward and a faggot and there's nothing I can do about it.

Therapist: That's a lot to think about.

Elliot: You asked for it.

Therapist: Yes, I did.

Elliot: I never have just listened to my own thoughts, but I am surprised at what I am thinking about. To be honest with you, I think a lot of the fear I have of being viewed as a gay person is that people will confront me and I will have to do something back to them. That really is my big problem. Of course I still think I am a piece of shit anyway. But my biggest problem is that I feel like I have to do something if people make fun of me. I am not really a good fighter. If I say something back, it might cause a fight. It's pretty much a problem with standing up for myself. If I didn't think people would fight me, it would be a different thing altogether.

Therapist: Is that our only option? Fight or be a coward?

Elliot: I suppose.

Therapist: Could we do anything else?

Elliot: We can always do something else.

Therapist: What thoughts would you have to give up, to do something differently, something that you would be content with doing? If you had one wish that would help handle this situation, what would it be?

Elliot: That they would burst into flames?

Therapist: That's one option. How about something that is more related to you and your thinking.

Elliot: I'm not sure what to do. That's why I came here. This is sort of the same thing my dad did. He didn't say I was a faggot, but he might as well have.

Session Seven

Therapist: Can you ever be just one thing?

Elliot: I guess not.

Therapist: We may very well be a combination of a lot of things, both good and not so good.

Elliot: Yes, that's true.

Therapist: It's one thing to say it's true. It's another thing to believe that it's true.

Elliot: I understand, sort of.

Therapist: It looks to me like if someone insults us, we make ourselves entirely bad. Like when your father rejected you and you became a piece of shit. You all of a sudden became unacceptable. Then your imaginary person called you a faggot, and you became that thing. It's like there is a magic wand that makes you bad. Is there one that makes you good?

Elliot: Yeah, when people praise me. Then I think I'm good.

Therapist: Until someone tells you you're not?

Elliot: Yes.

Therapist: We may want to get hold of that. From where I'm sitting, it seems like it would be very exhausting.

Elliot: What do you suggest?

Therapist: I would suggest that you, first, begin to realize that you are neither good nor bad. You are a number of things, unequal in value and significance. You are too many things to be called by just one name. You can begin to view the things people say to you, both good and not so good, as suggestions. No more than suggestions.

Elliot: So, if someone tells me I am a no good, stinking rotten person. That is a suggestion?

Therapist: Of course. And it is a suggestion we can either accept or reject. Simply because someone believes this about us is not proof enough that it's true. If someone doesn't like us, is that enough evidence that we are unlikeable? It would be insane for us to believe it anyway. There is overwhelming evidence that it isn't true. It would be insanity to give this statement much more than that, an insane suggestion from a person who appears to have a very little grasp on reality.

Elliot: It's like they're crazy and they are ranting about crazy shit.

Therapist: That's another way of looking at it. And if we join in with it, we are acting insanely by accepting their insane reality.

Session Eight

Elliot: It's sort of like arguing with a crazy person.

Therapist: Yes, and would we want to fight a crazy person for saying crazy things to us?

Elliot: No. I would probably feel sorry for them.

Therapist: Let's use that same imagery to understand your father's response to you when you told him you are gay. Is there any connection you can make?

Elliot: My father isn't crazy. He is pretty sane, actually.

Therapist: Great! But was he saying some crazy stuff to you?

Elliot: Yes. He was saying that gay people are filthy, an abomination, disgusting, drug addicts, sex fiends and pedophiles.

Therapist: And what is sane about that?

Elliot: Nothing . . . unless I think it's sane to think that.

Therapist: Is it sane to think you are an abomination filthy, drug addicted, disgusting pedophile?

Elliot: It's pretty insane for someone to think that. I still don't like it.

Therapist: I'm glad you don't like it. I wouldn't expect you to like it.

Elliot: Well, how do I get rid of my anger?

Therapist: You can change your thoughts.

Elliot: Like thinking what he's saying is insane?

Therapist: How would you respond to an insane person who said these things to you?

Elliot: I get it.

Therapist: Good, but how would you respond? What would you tell yourself?

Elliot: I would tell myself that he doesn't know how to behave. He is hallucinating about something. He is saying things that are crazy and he can't help it.

Therapist: What emotion would you feel then?

Elliot: I guess I would feel sad. Maybe I would think it was funny.

Therapist: Shame on you.

Elliot: Is that a suggestion?

Therapist: Very funny.

Session Nine

Therapist: We're coming to the end of our session. This is where I like to get some feedback, just to make sure we are on the same page. Tell me what we talked about today. Or, better yet, tell me what you remember most about your session.

Elliot: Most? I think when you said, 'We cannot have contentedness in our lives unless we are loved and respected by everyone we meet?'

Therapist: What about that interests you?

Elliot: Sometimes I think I cannot be as content as I'd like to be unless people appreciate me and respect me. Like it's the end of the world, if someone doesn't like me. I just wish I could do more about that.

Therapist: It isn't easy, but you can.

Elliot: If you could help me with that, I would really appreciate it.

Therapist: What do you tell ourselves, say, when someone thinks you behaved badly?

Elliot: Tell myself?

Therapist: Yes, listen to your mind. It tells us our beliefs. It will tell you what you think of certain things. Let's say someone treated you rudely, say at the convenient store. Say the cashier talked on her cell phone and didn't treat us very well, as a customer. What would you tell yourself about that?

Elliot: I would tell myself she was rude.

Therapist: And . . . ?

Elliot: She shouldn't be?

Therapist: And . . . ?

Elliot: She should change.

Therapist: Why?

Elliot: Because I want her to?

Therapist: What if she doesn't change?

Elliot: She would be a horrible person and I couldn't stand that.

Therapist: So you couldn't live contentedly while she was in the world acting rudely?

Elliot: Now I get it.

Therapist: If our contentedness depends on how well people cooperate with our wishes, we are likely to be discontented a lot of the time.

Elliot: I get that part, but what can I do instead.

Therapist: Remember how we talked about viewing the situation differently?

Elliot: About seeing people who act strangely as insane?

Therapist: Sure. If the cashier were viewed as crazy, what kind of behavior would you expect from her?

Elliot: Crazy?

Therapist: Should crazy people act any differently?

Elliot: I guess not.

Therapist: Put that in your own words.

Elliot: I can still be content in my life, even if people are acting crazy and saying crazy things. I don't have to fight anyone or yell back at them. I can think, 'Boy, this person is really making a lot of poor choices. They are saying all sorts of crazy shit and behaving strangely. I think I should just move away from them.'

Therapist: What about your thoughts concerning being gay?

Elliot: I guess I still feel like it would be better to be straight.

Therapist: Can you be content in your life if you're not like other people?

Elliot: Sure I can. I just have to stop thinking that just because someone thinks something bad about me that it's true. I have to give myself my own value, rather than taking everyone's random suggestions of my value. I am in charge of the way I feel because I am in charge of the way I think. If I think differently, I will feel differently. I will never like it that people don't like me because I'm gay, or any other reason. But I certainly can live my life and be content. Yes, I it will take the force of will; but I think I can do that.

Chapter Nine
Mano Po Must Never Die

I'm a watcher; an observer; a mental note–taker. Unlike birding in an aviary, where the brightest colors often get the most attention, I regularly focus on the simplest people. They have the most to say to me. Starbucks is ideal for watching people.

I stood in line, watching and listening as an Asian boy and girl ordered two large Starbucks. They moved to the side and waited to receive their coffees from the barista. The boy was dressed in all the latest gear, white tank top, hat to the back, jewelry, pants hanging down past his butt, blue Joe Boxers, utterly visible, chains, the works. The girl wore equally trendy clothing, pink Converse sneakers, skinny jeans, a tribal arm tattoo and various facial piercings.

I was more taken by the contrast between the cool, rough–neck, hip–hop look the boy was desperately trying to preserve as he delicately sprinkled cinnamon onto his Grande coffee in a venti cup with two pumps hazelnut, two pumps vanilla, two pumps caramel, two Equals and four Sweet'N Low, filled to the top with cream, extra cream on the side, double cupped with no sleeve, a stir stick and stopper in the top.

I carried my plain, black coffee to an empty table in the food court, sat down and reminisced on my own life as a teen. Over the rim of my cup I spied an Asian man sitting pensively at a table nearby, his black–gray hair neatly combed and flipped like an ocean wave in the front. He was dressed in traditional, Western clothing, but was also wearing a barong. We locked eyes, but quickly looked away, recovering smoothly from our accidental encounter.

He was with a young girl who I imagined was his daughter. The two sat together, not talking. The girl was a bit jumpy, anticipatory, looking from side to side and checking her phone for texts, the sleeves of her shirt half–covering the palms of her hands. Before long the man reached around and took out his billfold and carefully removed some paper money; he handed it to the girl, and she bolted toward Starbucks, taking her place at the back of the line. She gave two small, excited jumps, outwardly energized by some inner thought she was having. Her movements were quick, rapid, unlike her father who seemed to move in slow motion, as if performing tai chi, adjusting his chair, settling in contentedly, folding his arms over his chest and crossing one leg over the other.

It wasn't long before the girl recognized the boy and girl I had been observing earlier. The jumpy girl apparently knew the pink Converse girl because, when they saw one another, they initiated an animated, dance–like greeting, gripping each other's forearms. The boy stood apathetic, sipping his coffee, cinnamon on his upper lip, focused on maintaining his emotional distance. The jumpy girl pointed in the direction of her father. Both girls waved. The man smiled back.

Not long after, the girl, followed by her friends, carried two coffees to the table where her father sat. The hip–hop boy put down his coffee and approached the man. His young–and–free–to–be–me demeanor suddenly changed and he was, instead, solemn, deferent. There wasn't a trace of the youthful self–indulgent overconfidence he was showing only minutes before. The boy moved toward the older man, greeted him and called him *Uncle*. The boy reached for the man's hand and raised the man's fingers to his own forehead. The boy bent his knees ever so slightly, as if genuflecting. The Converse girl waited her turn and did the same.

The boy and the girl stood quietly with their hands folded over their midsections, listening while the older man spoke softly to them. When he had finished talking, the teens stepped backward and resumed their conversation with the jumpy girl.

I imagined that I must be in the presence of royalty, or at least someone who was very wealthy or possibly famous – someone who *deserved* this level of respect. I looked at his ring finger, expecting to see a wide, ostentatious red ruby. He wore only a simple watch and a gold band on his left ring finger. The boy and his friend chatted with the jumpy girl, but soon left, bowing their heads once more in the man's direction.

Who was this person?

Was he a holy man?

A superstar perhaps?

Should I ask for his autograph?

I decided to keep an eye on him.

* * * * *

My own father wasn't quite as composed and patient as the man in the barong. Neither did he have a whimsical hair flip. Instead he had a severe military–style crew cut. He never hit or spanked me, but he could bark out orders so rapidly I would freeze, not hearing a single word he was saying, for fear of missing something. I can still remember how he taught me to tell time or to solve a math problem, aggressively asking me if I understood - yet. I have no memory of anything he said; just a clear picture of his flaring nostrils and the sharp texture of his spiky hair.

* * * *

Like most of us, my social-emotional learning began with my parents, my father's threatening nostrils, my mother's Catholic guilt; but later, the number of my social-emotional learning trainers grew to include my teachers, relatives, other adults, peers and the media, a broader selection of people from a wider spectrum of life, each of whom helped to shape what would later become my worldview and my emotional range.

Social emotional learning seems to be a fundamental human ambition, an innate human drive to discover and practice the rules for fitting in, for being more like others, for being viewed as normal, one of the crowd. Social emotional norms dictate how much and under what circumstances emotional behavior is acceptable. Schizophrenia, for example, is a mental health condition that is believed to be an extreme deviation from the social-emotional norm. On an island where everyone has schizophrenia, however, visitors without the condition would be viewed as abnormal and in need of medication.

As most of us know, Rudolph the Red Nosed Reindeer had a very shiny nose, a nose that deviated quite a bit from the social norm. Because of this condition, he was excluded by all the other reindeer from all the reindeer games. Feeling dejected and unloved, Rudolph wandered about, telling himself he was no good, seeking a place where he could just live out his life, in isolation, free of ridicule. Rudolph found himself on the Island of Misfit Toys.

Rudolph the Red Nosed Reindeer and the Island of Misfit Toys is a story intended to provide people, particularly children, with hope by suggesting that social norms are not fixed but, instead, can be improved upon if we could all just agree to broaden the definition of what is deemed *normal*. To make the point, Rudolph uses his handicapping condition, his nose, to guide Santa's sleigh through the fog. Likewise, his new friends, the misfit toys, begin to reveal their individual value by demonstrating their unique talents, in spite of their differences. The Abominable Snowman proves his worth by placing the star on the Christmas tree and the dentist-elf is elevated to sainthood after fixing a toothache. Each of the characters, after proving their worth, finds someone normal who is actually willing to play with them, in spite of their imperfections.

Similarly, these same norms can impact social-emotional learning and emotional health by regulating such things as access, freedom and gender roles. It is repeatedly said that males don't cry. Females, on the other hand, have traditionally been viewed as the more emotional, sensitive sex. In the past, females were habitually portrayed in media as easily distraught, fainting into the arms of a strong, more resilient male. Even today, women are shown as having little control of their emotions, frequently striking people, particularly males, without repercussion, ostensibly because they are far too undisciplined, silly and arbitrary to know better.

Television and film often show disciplined males keeping order and giving clear and competent direction, while women seek support and approval from them. Women who prove themselves redeemable under these circumstances are normally those who acquire more masculine traits, while still maintaining their femininity. These portrayals, we may assume, are assimilated into the developing characters of growing young women.

Although there is widespread belief that women are more emotive, passionate and weepy, a study at Vanderbilt University found that men and women possessed equal potentials for emotional expression, equally sensitive, equally distant, equally impersonal and equally passionate. Emotion, it appears, is essentially sexless, a tool whose contour, dexterity and acuity are shaped over time by the unique experiences each of us has within a given culture.

Social emotional learning is a trial and error process of behaving, reviewing and assessing results; a sharpening of the skills we are always drawing upon for effectively cooperating and collaborating (and eventually copulating) with others.

One's competence in emulating emotional custom, ritual and ceremony has an impact on how well we fair as members of a society. Rudeness, for example, can be intentional or unintentional, depending on one's awareness of or appreciation for the social custom in which the behavior is observed.

Behaviors that are considered polite or rude frequently vary from place to place. The Russian language, for instance, does not include the same civilities, courtesies and considerations as the English language; so when Russian is translated directly from Russian to English, it can sound rather rude to an English speaker and listener. In China, few people if any line up and take turns as we do in Western cultures. Most Chinese choose, instead, to push and shove their way to the front, showing very little if any Western-style courtesy or emotional constraint. Ticket booths and train stations that cater to tourists have begun constructing metal fences, similar to stockyard panels, to force people to line up in front of the money–taker /ticket–seller; but, short of these accommodations, there are few native Chinese willing to stand in line, and it is not considered rude in China not to do so.

* * * *

Social emotional learning, custom and ritual have always fascinated me, making my experience at Starbucks with the Asian man and his daughter all the more enjoyable. Seconds after the two teens left the food court, the man and the girl stood to leave. The girl was still quite excitable. I watched as the older man rose confidently and pushed his chair neatly under the table. He looked at his daughter in a manner that prompted her to push in her own chair. The man collected the trash from the tabletop and handed the girl her own empty cup to throw away. She accepted it without protest and dropped it into the bin.

Once on their way out, the older man placed his hand lightly on the young girl's shoulder and the bounce in her step seemed to slow a bit, while her father's own step slightly quickened. The two found a balanced cadence, a tempo with which they could both walk comfortably together. They disappeared into the crowd.

Later that day I searched Google for some information on what I had seen happen between the man and the trendy teens at Starbucks when they touched the man's fingers to their foreheads and genuflected. I discovered what I had witnessed was a Filipino greeting called *Mano Po*, *mano* meaning hand; *po* is placed at the end of a sentence when addressing elders.

I learned that Filipino children and young people greet or say goodbye to their elders by taking the right hand of the elder with their own right hand and touching the back the elder's hand lightly on their forehead.

Mano Po is apparently a Filipino custom for showing respect to elders and receiving their blessing. This gesture of deference is not, as I had supposed, reserved for the wealthy, the famous or the politically connected. *Mano Po* is performed as a sign of respect with all elders by Filipino youth, regardless of their status or social class.

In Filipino culture, aging people evoke sincere and reverential emotions and behaviors from younger, less experienced people. How magnificent to live long enough to be honored for enduring this short, yet chaotic journey called life? To be prized for one's experience and knowledge; to have achieved an even higher degree of personal value and social significance as a consequence of normal aging.

In my lifetime, older people have never been greeted with any particular degree of enthusiasm. It seems, instead, after a certain age, older people become more or less invisible, incidental, imaginary and tedious, much like the appreciation we show when cleaning the underside of a toilet bowl. We know the underside is there and we know it needs attention, so we pay attention to it now–and–then, just to keep up appearances. The aging person, placed under these harmful psychological pressures, can, instead of the gift of *Mano Po*, expect aging to be a frightening period, more likely a time for dread, even terror and less an opportunity for experiencing a sense of achievement and self–acceptance.

It is my best judgment that the gesture of *Mano Po* exists to ensure that there will always be a wealth of social-emotional knowledge passed from one generation of Filipinos to another, to ensure the survival of their culture, making the essential acts of collaboration, cooperation and copulation between members of this civilization a real and lasting possibility.

Mano Po is a gesture that represents hope, symbolizing a striking contrast to the people with whom I have become accustomed to knowing in my own culture, people who shout orders and demands at one another, swear, discuss intimate and private matters on national television, people who celebrate their fortieth birthdays surrounded by black crape and Styrofoam grave markers, people who cough into the open air, shoot one another over a parking space, push, pull, grab and generally behave selfishly and inconsiderately. People who I believed, before discovering the clues to improved emotional intelligence, *made* me feel angry and anxious. Now I am aware of *Mano Po* and its potential to influence my own thinking about how I encounter others and how I imagine myself as I grow older. It will take the force of will to do that.

Chapter Ten
Who's In Control?

Why is it that some of us grow into emotionally competent adults, supporting intimate and social relationships, while some struggle in their simple connections with others? Could the secret be in our genetic makeup? Culture? Some irregularity in our social-emotional learning? The concept of emotional intelligence and its role in our ability to live contentedly with ourselves and others has emerged as one potential answer.

Emotional intelligence refers to our individual capacity to perceive, control, evaluate and monitor our own feelings and emotions and those of others. Improvement in emotional intelligence, therefore, must start with an assessment of those attributes that are believed to contribute to emotional intelligence.

Discovering our *locus of control*, or how strongly we believe we have control over how we view the situations and experiences in our lives, and how much control we have over them, can provide valuable insight.

* * * *

The term *locus of control* was first introduced in the 1950s by psychologist Julian Rotter. There are believed to be two classifications of thought using Rotter's theory:

* *Internal* and *External Locus of Control*

Gauging our own locus of control from the perspective of improved emotional intelligence may be as simple as asking and answering these questions: Are my emotions a product of what happens to me? (External) Or am I responsible for creating my own emotions through perception, appraisal and thinking? (Internal)

People with an internal locus of control tend to be self–reliant and believe that they are responsible for outcomes, including the emotions they express in relation to the events they experience, both good and bad. People with an internal locus of control tend to view their emotions as a result of their own efforts.

People with an external locus of control tend to be more negative about others, themselves and their place in the world. Those with an external locus of control believe that forces outside of themselves affect their emotions and their ability to successfully manage emotion through improved thinking and perceiving. They tend to stake their futures on things such as fate, luck, god or society. People with an external locus of control (and those in most need of improvement in emotional intelligence) tend to view events and other people as the source of their emotional state:

Emotionally intelligent people traditionally express a clear and obvious internal locus of control in how they encounter others. Emotionally intelligent people seek to improve, even if they fail at achieving their goals; but they don't seek to be perfect. They accept their fallibility and very–human potential for success and failure, strengths and weaknesses.

Unlike the story of *Rudolph and the Island of Misfit Toys* discussed in the previous chapter, improved emotional intelligence is not a process of proving to others that one is worthy of acceptance and approval, rendering the story of Rudolph and his friends the antithesis of what improved emotional intelligence is expected to represent.

We can accept ourselves even if we are not accepted by others. Emotionally intelligent people do not seek to demonstrate their goodness by displaying their talents and skills, hoping for applause and approval. Emotionally intelligent people seek to build *self–acceptance* in place of approval from others. Self-acceptance is an individual's satisfaction or happiness with oneself, and is thought to be necessary for good mental health. Self- and other-acceptance involves self-understanding, a realistic, albeit subjective, awareness of the imperfections inherent in ourselves and others. When we're self– and other-accepting, we acknowledge all facets of ourselves and others, strengths and weakness, successes and failures, not just the positive, more esteem–able parts, but all of it.

* * * *

Emotional intelligence theory stresses that true self–worth is not a product of how we are treated by others. On the contrary, our idea of human dignity cannot rely solely on how consistently and reliably others show us respect or express approval of our behavior. *Mano Po*, for instance, the Filipino custom previously discussed, although extraordinarily uplifting, should never be viewed as a replacement for self– and other-acceptance. In its magnificent simplicity, *Mano Po* makes experience and strength a dynamic of our dreams for the future; but it cannot become a replacement for our own ability to form our own rational, balanced judgments about ourselves and others – which can be fair, kind, hopeful and forgiving.

We must seek to improve our emotional intelligence by strengthening our dependence on our own logic, reason and, above all, ourselves for a truer measure of the worth we place on ourselves and others. We can never forget that each of us holds intrinsic value, simply because we are human and will likely fail throughout our lives. We can, if we try, live contentedly with that knowledge.

* * * *

We've discussed the idea that we have a tendency to externalize (external locus of control) the source of our emotions and expect emotional and behavioral change from others, rarely from ourselves. We have a tendency, as well, to make negative and critical whole person evaluations of others who do not cooperate with our expectations of them.

I once had a client who made himself unhappy when he went into a store to buy something. He told himself: *Cashiers and store people should greet me when I come into the store. They didn't and that makes them bad people. Store people should be kind and courteous when I place my food order. They aren't, so that makes them assholes. Store people should thank me after I pay. They don't, so they are bad and should be fired and live a miserable and thankless existence.*

This level of self- and other-evaluation is too critical and fuels the process of expressing anger, preventing the expression of more balanced, life–sustaining emotion. This method of emotional problem–solving also denies the existence of human imperfection. Essentially, if someone does something we don't like, we believe that they are entirely bad for having done it.

Anxiety is frequently generated from focusing on the negative aspects of an experience and forming negative expectations of similar, future experiences. If we expect perfection, we will be disappointed each time that standard is not met. Self–talk, as we discussed in previous chapters, can create an *expectancy* of some preconceived outcome; what may be called anticipatory anxiety.

My client decided to do something about his anticipatory anxiety when going into stores. He was tired of making himself angry over magical thinking and his idea that he couldn't stand it when people didn't behave as he expected. He chose to practice on the counter person at his physician's office.

He imagined that the counter woman would not greet him, as she normally didn't. Even worse, she would ask him questions about his personal medical condition by shouting them across the waiting area. His first step was to change his self–talk: *What am I afraid of, when counter people are rude to me? What does it mean about me if counter people are rude to me? Am I the only person on the planet who experiences hardship? What do I say to myself when I think of counter people and their behavior toward me?*

* * * *

Self–talk is the language we use to communicate with ourselves about everything within our perception. Self–talk is part of our thinking process made into behavior. As we are presented with problems, or decisions, we draw on our familiarity with them by reflecting on past experiences and tell ourselves how we solved the problem in the past. Irrational self–talk prevents us from effectively solving our problems. Rational self-talk is likely to help us resolve our issues, based on fact and efficiency. *Am I telling myself that if counter people treat me as if I am worthless, that I am worthless? What am I afraid of?*

Self–talk is repetitive, words and phrases we grow accustomed to telling ourselves. Our inner language can be rational or irrational, imaginative or scientific. These automatic thoughts are a result of analysis and problem–solving that has taken many years to establish in our brains – learned over time through repeated experience. We don't often search for evidence that contradicts our self–talk. We rely on how we talked to ourselves the last time the same or similar situation arose and we handle it in the same way.

Improving one's emotional intelligence requires that we interfere with this specific activity, if it doesn't result in our contentedness. We have to become aware of what we tell ourselves and we have to be ready to challenge what we tell ourselves using a more rational, science-based perspective. *It certainly doesn't mean I'm worthless if counter people are rude toward me. It doesn't mean anything about me, in truth. I can be content even if people are not friendly toward me. I won't be happy about it, but I can accept that people act this way. I can be content even when things don't go the way I would like them to go.*

* * * *

Changing our self–talk is a time–consuming task, requiring a lot of effort and cognitive vigilance. Even those who have spent a lifetime trying to establish a fact–based process for improving emotional intelligence cling to some of their old, faulty beliefs. Ideally, people's beliefs should evolve as they gain new experiences; but that isn't always the case. We have to keep in mind that we spent our entire lives building the beliefs we now hold. Dismantling them today will not be possible. It will take a great deal of time and effort. We might start that process today, however.

* * * *

I have developed for myself a system of self-talk that works for me. I simply say to myself: *Shit is shit and I can be content when shit is shit.*

Shit does not have to be cake for me to be content. Shit can be shit and I know that at some point shit will be consumed by time and I can live contentedly while that happens. Essentially, shit is time-limited and I can wait, and I will be content in the meantime.

* * * *

What does it mean to give up an established belief for a new one? Simply, no new belief will ever be accepted without first wrestling, to some degree, with an already–established belief. And established beliefs prevail, even when the beliefs act against our own self–interests. After all, beliefs are our personal laws, our expectations of others, our worldview. Our beliefs guide our decision–making and give us a sense of justice. To improve our emotional intelligence, however, we must break our own internal laws and discover new ideas, establish more flexibility in our beliefs.

"She is such an asshole. She should be more caring of me! She doesn't treat anyone well."

"What evidence do you have for that belief?"

"Evidence? I don't have any evidence. I just believe it. It's not a bad belief. It's a good thing to care about people."

"She obviously doesn't hold that belief. If you really thought people should care about each other, you would be caring of her now, rather than ridiculing her for not behaving the way you demand."

* * * *

Our current emotional life is guided by our experiences, reinforced over time by repetitive, cyclical thinking. Our early encounters with our family, friends, teachers and neighbors contributed to how we now face the world. The stories we were told and the customs we were trained to embrace each supplied us with what we believe is an emotional and behavioral norm. We are now left with having to preserve our current way of thinking, the way we've been trained, or to challenge some of things we were taught and to do something new.

It won't be easy to change the way we think and behave, but it is possible. We will discuss the methods we can use to begin this process in subsequent pages. For now, straddling the chasm between our current beliefs and building and reinforcing new, more productive beliefs will present us with our most arduous challenge for improving our emotional intelligence. It will take the force of will to do that.

Chapter Eleven
Magical Thinking

I hope to talk about the topics of wishful–ness, fairytales and magical thinking, particularly the confidence some of us have in communicating with gods and deities to help solve our emotional problems.

We discussed the idea of magical thought in a previous chapter – the idea that our feelings come from how people treat us, as if we are somehow under a spell that not only provokes us to feel, but sustains our emotional state. Our discussion in this chapter will focus on clarifying our dependence on spirits, ghosts and other fantastic beings that we have come to believe influence our destiny and our emotional life. We should know beforehand, however, that this is not a discussion of the truth or untruth in the existence of god. It is a discussion of how we use and misuse the idea of god to resolve our emotional problems in that way.

Wishful–ness and magical thinking rely on finding causal relationships between events, particularly in nature, even when scientific information says there are none. Wishing and magic are the stuff of great fiction and, unto themselves are quite harmless. In fact, magical thought and wishful–ness are responsible for multiples of millions of smiles, tears and joys and holds an important place in the world of entertainment. The exclusive use of wishful–ness and magical thinking, however, as they relate to the expectation of benefit, recompense or relief from pain and suffering can inhibit our reliance on our own skills and abilities to overcome our own hardships, resulting in a weakening of our emotional intelligence.

Many religious people rely on prayer in hopes of conjuring a miracle when they experience significant problems in their lives. Others will pray for less immediate reasons, asking divine intervention for such things as winning the lottery or hitting a homerun. While prayer and meditation have shown to play an important role in calming the body's response to stress, these activities cannot be confidently relied upon to pay the rent, improve our Internet speed or help us get that job. Nor can they be trusted to bring harm or bad luck to our enemies.

"His troubles are his karma."

"Step on a crack, break your mother's back."

"Pray! God will take it all away."

"Allah will settle the score."

"Leave it in the hands of God."

Emotionally intelligent people appreciate the fact that regardless of who or what we choose to attribute our actions, goals and purpose, we are each responsible for everything we do, including the choice to be helpless and always in the hands of fate to achieve our emotional goals. It is up to each of us to give meaning to our own lives. Meaning and personal responsibility are imbedded in the choices we make. Some of us choose to be powerless; but even then we remain responsible for that choice. In the long run, we shape ourselves and, thereby, shape our lives. That process can only end at the moment of our death; but the choices we make before that mystical day are ultimately our own responsibility.

* * * *

Emotional intelligence theory does not reject the existence of gods and deities, nor does it support or reject atheism or agnosticism. Emotional intelligence theory, in fact, comfortably accommodates all concepts of both god and godlessness. Emotional intelligence theory, however, does reject the idea that our emotional health can be influenced by luck, gods, curses, karmic retribution or devil's play. Emotional intelligence theory supports the idea that improved emotional intelligence is achieved by accepting that our unfortunate circumstances are normal, natural and explainable events, all manageable and all of them time limited.

Magical thinking can hinder the true potentials of the human mind and may actually impede improvement in emotional intelligence. Emotional intelligence theory posits that our mental state is influenced by perception, appraisal and thinking – applying *meaning* to the events we experience. *Perception* and *meaning* are not products of gods and deities but, instead, products of thought. For thought to be life–enhancing, it must be subject to reality testing, revision and clarification. Fixed, dogmatic beliefs are not matters open to revision, leading those who choose to maintain these beliefs with an over–reliance on magical thought to resolve their emotional issues.

Not every magical thought, mind you, should be subject to scientific scrutiny. On the contrary, some magical thinking is useful, doesn't result in hardship and is rather manageable. What, for example, would love, film and Christmas be without a little magical thinking and wishful–ness? There may, in fact, be a bit of magical thinking in my belief that I am conscious; that a mouse is smarter than an elephant; or that improved emotional intelligence will result in emotional well–being. These beliefs are all quite manageable without the use of science to prove them. Conceivably, at some point, however, additional knowledge or a change in context may render these beliefs false; but I currently have no need to examine them.

* * * *

Although I am quite fond of emotional intelligence theory, especially as it relates to how science can help to improve perception, I must admit that, even today, I maintain some magical thoughts that may not exactly improve my life. After all, I have been a member of the human race a lot longer than I have been practicing emotional intelligence theory. (We will later learn that the influence of repetition on neural coding requires a bit of time and effort to undo.)

I sometimes give magical evidence to support my belief in an afterlife, for example, and attribute, to some degree, my successes to god's favor. *Thank God for that!* While I'm at it, I will admit that when I find myself alone, I wonder what my mother and other dead relatives are up to at that particular moment in time, all pretty much harmless; but all worthy of reconsideration, nonetheless.

Death appears to be one human experience to which many of us apply some kind of magical thought. My own beliefs in an afterlife seem to contribute to my motivation to achieve my goals and heighten my awareness of others, particularly in the matchlessness of what each person I meet has to teach me. Magical beliefs in a god and an afterlife, however, can produce a much different result.

I once met a woman whose husband suddenly died. "When my husband went to be with God," she said, "this bluebird came and sat on my porch rail. There is no explanation for it. It was late fall, when all the birds had flown south and this bluebird just appeared out of nowhere. So, anyway, it sat there for a moment and then it looked me straight in the eye and I could tell it was Jesus trying to tell me something. So I opened my heart and I listened. You know what Jesus said? He said that my husband still loved me and that he was waiting for me in Heaven. Jesus said that my husband was thinking about me and was watching over me. That's why I collect blue birds. They remind me that my husband truly loves me and that he will come back. God works in such mysterious ways."

The woman's entire house was filled with statuettes of bluebirds. Stuffed animals, light fixtures, plates, switch covers, rugs and stained glass windows, all ordered over the telephone from the Home Shopping Network, were piled everywhere, each resembling a bluebird. She spent her days sitting in a La–Z–Boy recliner, because there was hardly a place to sit or sleep elsewhere. She did not leave the house and had lost contact with her friends and relatives. With her limited income, she tithed to a television church ministry, because the minister said he knew someone in his viewing audience was grieving for their lost husband and she knew it had to be her. "My husband is here. He is all I need, until I'm called home to be with him," she said. Her husband had been dead for fifteen years.

My own magical beliefs in an afterlife contributed to my understanding of this woman and actually helped me hear and learn from her. Her magical beliefs, by contrast, however, contributed very little to improving her human condition and may have resulted in shortening her life.

* * * *

I am comfortable using the word spiritual to identify my belief in what may be termed *the orchestration of human existence*. My spirituality, however, lacks a finite, absolute definition. For me, spirituality contains core beliefs in the values of social justice, fairness, honesty and human understanding. These core beliefs do not conflict with science, but are, instead, consistent with the principles of effective human cooperation, collaboration and copulation. I rely on the flexibility of my mind to think and reason beyond a fixed doctrine, two key features of improved emotional intelligence.

I like to imagine that there is meaning and purpose in human existence. I believe that meaning cannot be prescribed but is, instead, a product of being present when life provides me with potential clues. Unlike the barriers to free thinking that are often found in organized religion, spirituality provides me with an opportunity to evolve and even change what I think and believe, as I grow and learn. Above all, spirituality encourages me to believe in myself and my own potential, replacing dependency on religion with the possibility of ideas, notions, philosophies and viewpoints that will remain as alive, growing and vibrant as I allow myself to be.

The concept of spirituality helps me imagine how I might fit into some greater cosmic scheme of things. Of course there is no science to support my questions about why I am here or what happens after I die; but seeking answers to those questions from the perspective of open–mindedness and being in harmony with others, actually improves my life and the lives of the people with whom I come into contact. I may or may not discover the meaning of my life; but it will be my spirituality, not religion, that will make meaning more imaginable. While I search for answers to this and other unanswerable questions, spirituality will continue to influence my appreciation of beauty, love and creativity, things that seem to reveal some level of influence beyond the observable world.

**** **

In the final scene of the story *The Wizard of Oz*, Dorothy learns an unexpected truth from Glinda the Good Witch – that the power to return home had always been in her control. She simply had to click together the heels of her shoes, an act symbolizing her freedom and independence to act on her own behalf. When the Scarecrow angrily asked why this critical information had not been revealed to Dorothy sooner, the wise witch laughed and said, "Because she wouldn't have believed me; she had to learn it for herself." Glinda goes on to explain that the power to get home, like the courage, wisdom and heart her friends were seeking, had always been within. They simply had to believe in themselves. By the same measure, our mind is capable of more than we likely will ever know. We simply have to step outside our comfort zone and acknowledge that potential and see where it takes me.

Our goal in improved emotional intelligence is to provide all people, regardless of their belief in a higher power, a sturdier foundation for the development of a functional reality, one that encourages the use of personal judgment, reasoning and rational thought to resolve emotional problems. If, however, we resign ourselves to the whim and will of mystical powers, we are not likely to take full advantage of our own, innate power to achieve our human potential.

Emotional intelligence theory seeks an integrated, non–contradictory, reality–based system of emotional problem solving, one that includes a whimsical degree of magical thought and wishful–ness for good measure. It will take the force of will to do that.

Chapter Twelve
Intelligence

When my sister was born, she was clearly unusual. Her appearance, her distinctive facial and physical features were a curious, unexplainable phenomenon. I remember thinking, "Where did this baby come from? Whose baby is this?"

As an infant, my sister had dark, almost black, upturned eyes, a flat nose, a small mouth and large tongue. Her ears were curved inward. She had a single crease across both palms of her tiny hands, short stubby fingers, tiny feet with a larger than normal space between the big toes and the rest of them.

She was extraordinarily double-jointed, almost as if she had no bones at all. I didn't know that the features that gave my sister her unique appearance were the physical elements that made people with Down syndrome recognizable. Lying in her crib, I often peered in at her; she, staring into space, her dark eyes, like the black buttons that closed my winter coat, fixed on the musical mobile dangling above her head. I don't remember her ever crying or laughing or making any sound, really. She was always silent, lying on her back, occasionally moving her feet and hands.

For the first two years of her life, my sister couldn't roll over, sit-up or stand; and she couldn't talk. She shifted her position only minimally, often with help. Around three years, she started to roll over, sit up, maneuver herself onto all fours and sit in a chair without slumping into a bunch. She experienced some level of independence at around four years, scooting across the floor, propelling herself by thrusting her legs and feet forward and humping herself ever onward. She grew and developed in her own way, along her own timeline.

* * * *

In her teen years, she become much more self-aware and knew clearly that she was different. "I hate it," she told me one day as we prepared to go to her job at McDonald's. She cleared and wiped down tables and was overjoyed to do it. "I hate it," she repeated. She looked down at her lap, seemingly talking to herself. I reached to pull her seatbelt over her ever-expanding waistline. "Why?" I asked. "You like working there."

"They make fron' a me."

"Who?"

"The kids; the kids; make fron' a me." Her eyes magnified behind her thick glasses, smudged and always in need of a good cleaning, searched for answers in my face that, even if I could explain, would never really ring true for her.

* * * *

My sister survives on the belief that people are essentially good; and each time she experiences the recklessness of others, her expression is consistently a mix of deep sadness, regret and the hope that she will be forgiven for being unusual, so much unlike others that the most she could ever expect from them is to be forgiven.

All people with Down syndrome have some degree of intellectual disability and developmental delay. They are, however, far from being incapable of learning, especially to the degree that emotional expression, social expectation and the way in which others treat them as normal. People with Down syndrome are generally very sensitive to being a part of a social group. It is my best judgment that people with Down syndrome are commonly quite emotionally adept, genius at expressing affection toward others. The intellectual capacity of people with Down syndrome cannot be reliably predicted in infancy or early childhood, but the ability to express love and caring is often evident from a very early age. We may say that people with Down syndrome are seemingly pre-wired for expressing immense emotional intelligence.

* * * *

My sister entered school at around the same age as other children, only she spent her days in a room where the window in the door was covered with construction paper. I never saw her at recess, and we never sat together at lunch. Knowing her as I did, I could only imagine that she was content among her friends and teachers, never questioning the good intentions of those who were responsible for her care and education. She went from elementary, to junior and on to senior high school seated behind a window covered in construction paper. When she was twenty, she graduated from high school; and for all her efforts, she was mailed a diploma and a copy of her yearbook. Inside were an empty oval where her picture should have been and a barren, blank square where her biography might have been printed, if anyone had taken the time to gather the information from her.

Of course, when she got the yearbook in the mail, she leafed through it. She had no idea that her picture should be there, alongside the other members of her graduating class. She couldn't even have imagined such an honor. She was content to look over the familiar faces she remembered from school, the lunch lady, pictures of the abandoned hallways, the quad.

My mother, much less content, contacted the school and demanded that my sister be photographed and her picture sent by mail to everyone who had purchased a yearbook. Not only should there be a picture, but my mother strongly suggested that my sister's favorite color, her favorite song, her most commonly spoken phrase and her most cherished memory accompany the photo in exactly the same proportions as the oval and blank spaces that were provided to her classmates.

My sister was quite proud when she pointed out her own picture in the yearbook, after discovering it one day, glued perfectly within the spaces, as if it had always been there, proof that she was like everyone else. She looked up at me, through those damnable, smudged glasses, kissed her hand and brought it down on top of her own picture. "S'me," she said, "S'me." She laughed, extending her long tongue as she drew in more air to feed her belly laugh.

My sister has never been like anyone else, really. She is my cherished and pure spirit, someone who is never truly discontent for long or without a friend. Her life has been a hearty handshake, a warm and sincere hug and a promise for unconditional positive regard toward everyone she meets, no matter who they are or how they may have treated her in the past.

I can never imagine comparing myself to my sister's strength of character and her dedication to the idea that everyone possesses inherent goodness, if we just take the time to see it.

* * * *

The day I took my sister to her job at McDonald's, I tried to explain to her that evil people live in the world and that we have to simply accept their presence. As we pulled in to the parking lot, she pointed and said, "She's mean to me."

"Oh, *she's* the one," I said. "I'm going to tell her to leave you alone."

"She's pretty," my sister said.

"Pretty! She's a mean girl!"

"Oh go on," my sister said, "Be nice."

* * * *

My sister provided me with special education in emotional intelligence. From the day she was assimilated into our family and our neighborhood, complete with her own unique personality, her own strengths and her own weaknesses, she took every opportunity to become the strong-willed, sensitive and tremendously good-humored, highly emotionally intelligent woman she was, throughout her life.

* * * *

Intelligence is most frequently defined as the ability to learn or understand; what may also be referred to as intellect, an essential factor for working through new or difficult situations. An assessment of intelligence might include the capacity to apply knowledge gained from experience to manipulate one's environment through predictive and abstract thought.

General intelligence is believed (in the absence of disease or trauma) to be fixed, stable, unchanging over a lifetime. Some believe we are born with all the intellectual potential we will ever possess. There is, however, increasing discussion over the role *desire* and *tenacity* have on improving intellectual competence. Can we improve our intelligence through diligence and hard work?

Alas, because the concept of intelligence seems to be an arbitrary theory, made up of a number of unstable, evolving factors and ideas, most definitions of intelligence seem, ultimately, to alienate someone.

* * * *

Emotional intelligence may be the ability to identify, assess and control our own emotions, resulting in optimal mental health and overall physical well–being. Emotional intelligence may be a self–perceived measure, far more flexible and a lot more under our own control than general intelligence. For example, if we find that we're losing friends, jobs and family members, a decision to do something else, to explore other emotional options, is very much in the realm of possibilities. Unlike intellectual capacity, desire, effort and tenacity actually can play a role in improving emotional intelligence.

Emotional intelligence, in fact, doesn't appear to have an overly strong relationship to intellect. Some of the most skilled thinkers in the world can have little or no skill at emotional problem–solving, while people with Down syndrome can express genius in that same area.

Emotional intelligence is flexible, plastic and can be improved throughout life, depending on one's desire to improve. One simply needs to identify weakness in h/er emotional problem–solving skills and endeavor to improve upon them.

* * * *

The fabric of our emotional lives is an elaborate quilting of experiences. From the time of our birth, each square, each life experience, is stitched to the next to create the individuals we are today.

A keen awareness of our genetics and how our parents, relatives, friends and neighbors solved their own emotional issues, however successful, will provide insight into the fabric from which our own emotional intelligence is woven. How do we make judgments about the obstacles we face in our life? How do we overcome them? Each time we settle an emotional issue, are we choosing the quickest and most familiar option? Or do we put some effort into choosing from our emotional range? Do we forgive when we're not forgiven? Do we pardon when we're unfairly judged?

We've built our current level of emotional intelligence through a series of personal observations, trials and errors, punishments and rewards. And each time we apply our own unique emotional resolution to the same or a similar emotional event, we add strength to it. The more we repeat our current behaviors, the stronger and more predictable they become. Doing away with harmful, destructive and life–damaging behaviors takes the strength of a wrecking ball. Improvement in our emotional intelligence may require us to swing a wrecking ball at the voluntary contributions we make to our own unhealthy thinking and take them down, one by one. It will take the force of will to do that.

****

My sister's medical and cognitive impairments increased over the years and unraveled the mystery of her human condition more and more. From the day she came home from the hospital, wrapped in a yellow, satin edged blanket, she was the most wonderful gift I could ever have imagined receiving. *My sister Stacia died on her 52nd birthday, July 19, 2016.*

.

Chapter Thirteen
Murderers' Row

What purpose does emotion serve?

Emotion is believed to be a necessary element of communication for members of a particular culture or group. Naturalist Charles Darwin imagined that emotions are adaptations that allow both humans and animals to survive and reproduce. Emotional intelligence theory endorses this view.

Without some emotional frame of reference, we would not be capable of establishing trust with one another, an elemental component for building the at-ease atmosphere necessary for collaboration, cooperation and copulation among most species of animals, particularly humans.

There are hundreds of theories related to the number of emotions humans have the capacity to express. Paul Eckman suggests that the human face is capable of articulating more than 7,000 unique and distinctive expressions. Robert Plutchik's wheel of emotions identifies only eight basic feelings: joy, sadness, trust, disgust, fear, anger, surprise and anticipation.

Emotional intelligence theory, by contrast, proposes that there are two dominant human emotional potentials, *fear* and *attachment*, and that these two emotional potentials are used to regain, maintain or restore psychological and physical balance. Variations in these two emotions, i.e., sadness, joy, elation and anger are simply modulations, degrees in how we communicate fear and attachment. We might imagine two thermostats, one labeled *fear* and the other labeled *attachment*. The degrees of fear may include sadness, depression and dread, while the degrees of attachment may include such things as joy, illation, contentedness and love.

According to emotional intelligence theory, the expression of fear and attachment are natural, human emotional potentials. All other emotions are culture- and experience-specific, derivatives of fear and attachment and correlated with one's skill at operationally behaving as a member of a specific group.

The expression of fear and attachment can significantly change the body's chemistry, providing for the release of corresponding neurotransmitters, chemical messengers in the brain that modulate signals across synapses of brain cells and between other cells. For example, some of us will respond with fear if we are ridiculed. It is unlikely that being ridiculed will provoke the expression of attachment. We may believe that being ridiculed is potentially dangerous, harmful or threatening. To protect ourselves from this perceived danger and to regain homeostatic balance, we automatically activate our endocrine system (using thought alone) to release the stress hormones that will help sustain the fight-flight-or-freeze response required to make us safe and regain balance.

Stress hormones act by mobilizing energy from storage to muscles, increasing heart rate, blood pressure and breathing and shutting down metabolic processes such as digestion, reproduction, growth and immunity. That's why, when we are disrespected, teased, mocked or belittled we will feel a quick jolt of heat go up the back of our neck and our heart will begin to race. Our body is preparing itself to fight, flee or freeze and it only does that when we tell it we are in danger.

Most neurotransmitters are made from protein or its sub-units, amino acids. Serotonin, dopamine and GABA, for example, are neurotransmitters that are released when humans are feeling attachment, a positive, calm, content frame of mind, where there is a strong sense of well-being. When the neurotransmitters that produce a sense of calm are instead being overpowered by stress hormones such as adrenaline, cortisol and epinephrine, these messengers will have a significant impact on mood and behavior.

****

Emotion appears to vary to some degree from one culture to the next, from the family unit to the largest city, state and country. When we communicate to others that we are feeling content, sad, excited or frightened, we are giving them important information that they can then use to perceive our emotional state and to take action in relation to those culturally-defined emotional cues. Just as our own emotions provide valuable information to others, the expressions of those around us gives us a wealth of social information, as well.

Social emotional learning relies on a system of emotional turn–taking, a protocol for learning the consequences of one's behaviors as a member of a culture and storing that information away for when it's needed. How our behavior is normalized or rejected has a great deal to do with individual social-emotional learning.

****

My earliest and most powerful memory of social-emotional learning was of a little girl I met in elementary school. She was always dressed so well, little socks with tatted edges, hair in curls. She stood with the other little girls on the playground of the South Elementary school. She seemed to glow, the sun shining through her hair as she hung from the monkey bars, upside down, careful to keep her dress in place and her undies from showing. She would reach up to grip the bar, roll her knees and flip herself around, only to land perfectly on her two, immaculate patent leather shoes.

My first reaction to girls back then was to throw things at them, a rock, a burr, a cat. The burr I threw at this particular little girl is frozen forever in my mind. I pitched the burr at her, but it somehow travelled in slow motion and then clung to the fur ball that sat atop her woolen cap. We looked directly into one another's eyes, searching for some unspoken information, some sign of what to do next, drawing from our previous social-emotional learning experiences.

Getting nothing, we simply stared, anticipating one another. I was sure she would begin to cry and run to the teacher who stood checking her watch at the corner of the playground.

She didn't.

I began making up excuses in my head to tell the teacher that I would never have to use.

The little girl changed the game plan.

Astonishingly, she simply removed her hat, inspected my handiwork, pulled off the burr, smiled at it and handed it back to me. She wasn't happy about what had happened, nor was she angry. She was apparently content, smiling a simple yet mysterious smile.

I kept an eye on her.

As the school year progressed, I noticed that no matter what was happening around the little girl, she kept a smile on her face. Of course the other girls liked her, and the boys left her alone. There was nothing to be gained by needling, nettling, nudging, peeving, perturbing, pestering, plaguing, provoking, riding, riling, teasing, ruffling feathers or, notably, pushing her buttons. I was convinced that she was an alien, or a doll on a shelf that never changed its expression. I was most surprised that she wasn't afraid of me or my mischievousness. She treated me no differently than she treated anyone else. She didn't, it appeared, think I was a bad boy. I spent much of sixth grade sitting across from the little girl.

I sat on Murderers' Row, a special place for active (bad) children, always boys; a row of chairs and desks set aside especially, it seemed, for me. They didn't have anything like attention deficit hyperactivity disorder (ADHD) when I was a kid. At least no one knew about it if they did. There was no therapy or drugs or individual education plans. We didn't live in a culture where children were given diagnoses and *subscriptions* to amphetamines. I was just viewed by my teachers and most adults as an active, vigorous albeit bad boy who needed reining in.

On my second grade report card I am described as full of zip! and the class clown. In the absence of drugs to keep me in my chair, my teachers relied instead on old–fashioned ingenuity, patience and improved frustration tolerance; and, in the case of Murderers' Row, some misguided creativity.

The girl with the chronic smile sat nearby, always well–pressed, intelligent and content. I was in awe of her, never creating a disturbance, always a *good* girl. The teachers doted on her, and she always had a star, or a turkey, or an orange pumpkin on her forehead. I, on the other hand, when I wasn't sitting in Murderers' Row, spent the day slumped on a stool behind the piano, (occasionally not even worthy of sitting on Murderers' Row) wondering what sense it made for boys to have eyelids if they couldn't turn them inside out now and then.

Sitting behind the piano, while others were learning to read and write and solve arithmetic problems, it dawned on me that if I gave up headlocks, shooting spitballs and turning my eyelids inside out and smiled like the little girl, instead, I could improve my lot in life and the teachers (and maybe even the janitor) would like me and I would finally be a *good* boy. What I didn't realize is that I was about to add a new dimension to my previously established social-emotional learning customs.

I started smiling.

All the time.

I thought, "People are going to view me as good if it kills me."

My new smile was endearing me to no one. The lunch lady winced when she served me French fries, reaching her tongs toward me as if forking over a rattlesnake. At first, Mr. Travis, my teacher and the originator of Murderers' Row, did a double take and smiled back at me, confusedly. He checked his tie for gravy stains. If he had to turn his back and write on the board, he looked over his shoulder and checked on me, just in case. As the days progressed, Mr. Travis seemed to become more suspicious, even edgy, as if I were aiming something at him. Finally, one afternoon, he shouted over at me, "What! What! What's up? Wipe that grin off our face! You're making me nervous."

The little girl smiled at me over her shoulder.

I made up my mind then and there that I was destined to be forever *bad*. There was no hope. Once we are viewed as bad, there is just no amount of work that we could do to overcome that label. People would never fully accept me. In that case, I could never imagine to be viewed as good. How would I ever be good if no one would let me be good?

I settled in for a lifetime on Murderers' Row.

* * * *

Social-emotional learning might be defined as a product of the unique experiences we have with others within our environment. Although the term turn–taking is most often used to describe the rules in game–playing, it is also the model we might rely upon to cooperate with one another in our daily, social lives. Turn–taking, in a social context, consists of scripts, subtle signals, facial expressions, voice intonations and pragmatic rules learned over time, shaping our complex social rules and customs. We take turns expressing our thoughts and clarifying our meaning. We impose a level of cooperation and an expectation of collaboration between participants. Just as in game–playing, when a player breaks the rules or goes out of turn, the game is disrupted and the other players rebel, calling for a review of the rules to regain balance in the game:

"We aren't supposed to do that!"

"But I want to."

"That is totally against the rules. Stop it!"

"I do it all the time."

"Where did you learn that? Where were you raised?"

Throughout life we establish, through experience, the general principles for the expression of fear and attachment, resulting in a set of social constructs (rules) that start their development at birth and become the frame of reference we use to address most social situations. Social constructs represent meaning, a process of establishing a system for perception and cognitive/social verification. We internalize these rules of engagement, practice them and produce a system of social navigation:

*. *When you do this, we say 'Thank you.'*

*. *When someone does that, we express anger.*

*. *When this happens, we say, 'Excuse me.'*

*. *This is what boys do.*

*. *This is what girls do.*

*. *You are a bad boy! I will let you know when you're a good boy.*

*. *You are a good girl, but don't make a mistake because then you will be a bad girl.*

Voila! the creation of our personal, social-emotional learning handbook.

* * * *

Even today, when I walk through my old neighborhood and I pass that little girl's house sitting at the head of King Road, the one who smiled all the time and captured my attention for nearly four decades, I wonder why her smile could energize a room, while my own smile sent people seeking cover.

* * * *

Our personal, social-emotional learning handbook is an internal structure built from the dialogue we have with ourselves that consists of experience, a complex inner wisdom made up of words, phrases, body movements and gestures, meaning and perspective–taking. Most of us were emotionally trained in an environment of right and wrong, good and bad, best and better, where few alterations were allowed from what should and shouldn't be. It would have been a rare occasion for our social educators (parent, neighbors, relatives, teachers) to say, "Let's talk about the parts of our behavior that were right and the parts that were not right. Then we will compromise based on how they behave in France."

Our social educators trained us to behave properly in our own social environment – the sole determiners of the appropriateness of our behavior. They were also, by default, the sole determiners of our human worth, often referring to us as good or bad, depending on how well be adhered to their social-emotional instruction.

We learned that our human worth was not something we determined on our own, but was, instead, determined from somewhere outside ourselves; and we came away from it believing that emotional and social balance depended on receiving approval from others. Disapproval, of course, became our enemy.

＊＊＊＊

If you're like most of us, our early social emotion learning was a push toward getting it perfect; and we struggle to maintain that standard even today. When things are the way they should be, we believe we have balance. We believe we're living in a serene world where everything within our perception happens as it ought to. If our expectations are frustrated, when things are the way we believe they shouldn't be, we quickly go from balance to imbalance. Trying to maintain perfect balance in an imperfect world requires a steady state of caution and never–ending vigilance, resulting in nothing more than uninterrupted, continuous stress.

Weakened emotional intelligence can be detected in how regularly we rate ourselves and others as perfectly bad or perfectly good and things as magnificently awful for not meeting the ideal standard we set for how we believe the world must be. Our search for perfection and the ideal standard represents the emotional struggle within many of us, our neurotic attempt to hold ourselves and others to a benchmark of perfect rightness and perfect wrongness.

* * * *

Emotional intelligence theory speculates that to more fully appreciate how emotion is evolved in humans, we must also appreciate the cultural context in which social-emotional learning took place, the influence of the fight-or-flight-or-freeze response and the thoughts we produce in the moment to ensure the entire system of social-emotional evaluation remains unchanged.

* * * *

Our early social-emotional learning experiences, although very much a part of how we view ourselves and others at the moment, can evolve and change. As we experience life and broaden our exposure to a wider selection of people and ideas, we will likely encounter an assortment of contradictions to what we believed to be true and untrue, good and bad about ourselves and others. Nature has seen to that inevitability, providing humans with an abundance of potential for adapting to social and emotional variation. We just have to make ourselves available to Nature's gifts.

Our human mind is quite malleable, plastic and available for new information at any moment we choose to supply it. Reinventing our self-talk will go a long way to making that a real possibility. Each of us can, if we choose, break free from our own Murderers' Row, where we sit supporting the criticisms we receive from others, denying our uniqueness and validating our inadequacy and overall wickedness. Ultimately choosing to become someone we are not, a good or a bad person, to please the sensibilities and meet the expectations of the people around us. We can free ourselves from the idea that we must be perfect to be redeemable and, instead, seek to accept the unfixed inevitability of our future successes and failures.

* * * *

One morning, just as I stepped off the bus, I nearly ran straight into the little girl, standing there in her red coat with the black tooling and buttons, matching red beret sitting atop her ginger hair. We didn't speak. We only stared at one another, as had become our preferred way of communicating. She handed me a note, folded into a small, tight square. I was a little stunned. Sure, I got notes from my friends that read, *Eat shit*, or *I'll buy our bike*, or *I want to fight you after school*, but never a note from a girl. What could this note say? I didn't dare read it where anyone could see me. I slipped it into my back pocket and waited for school to be over.

* * * *

We can listen to our thoughts and become aware of our bodies. If we can feel our bloodstream flooding with stress hormones, and we are not being chased by a bear, then we are likely living on Murderers' Row and may seek, instead, to improve our emotional intelligence. It will take the force of will to do that that.

Chapter Fourteen
Perfectly Imperfect

Emotional wellness, much like the concept of emotional intelligence, can be described as a self–determined appraisal of one's own psychological well–being. How mentally healthy do we think we are? How much more mentally healthy would we like to be? How will we know when we're sane enough?

When it is an on–going practice, self–appraisal is believed to lead to heightened self–awareness. Self–appraisal, when it is done from a fair and rational perspective, inspires us to confirm or deny the foundation on which our own identity rests. Self– appraisal can be a thorny process indeed, as it prompts us to question the myths and fictions that often hold together the framework of our self–concept. Are we who we believe ourselves to be?

Many of us struggle to enjoy our day–to–day lives, partly because a large measure of our human value is supported by such things as what we do, what we have, what we look like and who notices. We compare ourselves to the archetypes we find all around us of good and bad, success and failure. Are we good enough? How do we know? Do we have to compare ourselves to others to gauge our own successes and failures? Weaknesses and strengths?

Our human value, it seems, is often an appraisal of ourselves in relation to others. After all, how would we know if our perceived talents and limitations were, in fact, positive or negative, good or bad without some comparison to other people? Is there some meaning in nature that describes such things as beauty, heroism, thoughtlessness, cowardice, wealth, success, ambition, intelligence and failure? These subjective notions cannot be verified in science and rely, instead, on how society defines them and how we, ourselves, accept them and then go about measuring up against them.

* * * *

Our idea of ourselves may be described as a set of schemas, organized patterns of thought that represent the relationships we have with ourselves and others. *Schema* means shape, or more generally, *plan*. Many of our self-schemas represent the shape of our self–image and embody our plan for ensuring that no contradictory information is ever allowed to interfere with that shape. *Schemata* are believed to be grounded in the present, but have a strong connection to our memories of our past. Our recollections of ourselves are generally biased in ways that tend to validate our self–schema while vigorously rejecting any information that conflicts with our affirming self–image. We might imagine a self– schema to be something like a puzzle representing a person's concept of what makes h/er both distinct and similar when compared to others.

Of course the *self* cannot be physically or scientifically detected. Instead, the self is a product of thought, convenient fictions that place each individual in the starring role in a world s/he has invented for h/erself. If the schema we use to establish our human value is weighted in how well we measure up to others, it can be said that our self–perception is externalized, meaning that we've lost control over our own ability to judge our own behavior and forfeited it to something or someone outside of our control, something like holding up a mirror to our own face and seeing the reflection of someone we don't know. If our image of ourselves is weighted so much in how we are perceived by others, it is likely that we are playing a role that does not truly reflect authenticity or the efficient use of our human emotional potential. We may, instead, possess a fragile, imaginary concept of ourselves, susceptible to being quite aggressive, deflecting guilt and shame, when our weaknesses are brought to our attention.

If we find ourselves behaving defensively when we are criticized, our response may indicate, instead, insecurity, fragility and less-than-optimal intrapersonal, psychosocial functioning. I am not suggesting that there is anything wrong with people who want to feel good about themselves. What I am saying is that feeling good about ourselves, when it is our prime directive, can result in excessive defensiveness and unsupported self-promotion. If we find ourselves somewhere in this description, our idea of self-esteem is likely quite fragile and may not provide us with any real, fact-based, rational psychological benefit.

* * * *

When the imaginative concept of self–esteem was first introduced to the world in the early to mid–1960s, people seemed to benefit from it. After all, the notion of self-esteem was intended to celebrate the revolutionary idea that humans are an amalgamation of flawed, less flawed and nearly flawless characteristics. According to the original concept of self–esteem, people are works in progress, neither good nor bad, wholly un–ratable.

Prior to the concept of self–esteem, society limited its personal rating system to a strict, puritanical, singular standard of success and failure, perfect and imperfect. The self–esteem movement offered an alternative to labeling oneself the sum totals of h/er most recent failings or victories. The idea of self-esteem posited that we could be a combination of traits, good and not–so– good, all at the same time and still retain human value!

Unfortunately, the theory of self–esteem proposed by Morris Rosenberg and other social–learning theorists has changed dramatically since the mid–1960s. Many of us have come to rely on the concept of self–esteem to compensate for our learned dependence on others for our personal value. Building self–esteem *now* is the practice of esteeming or prizing an image of ourselves, real or imagined, and vigorously protecting that image, even in the face of contradictory evidence. This twisted, unexpected use of the concept of self–esteem encourages us to rate ourselves in terms of our goodness and our acceptability in relation to other people – to identify an ideal and then to associate oneself with that ideal. The idea of self–esteem, however originally noble, is now more harmful than it is of any real value, simply because a truer accounting of ourselves must always include a reflection on our strongest and our weakest traits, our mediocrity and our brilliance, and then establishing some functional method for living comfortably with the sum total of that information.

* * * *

Most of us vacillate between being a good person and a bad person. We believe we are only as valuable as our last success. If we fail, we are a failure. If we win, we are a winner, but only until we lose again; at which time we will be, once again, a failure. By our own actions, we teach our children to be just like us and it all becomes a cycle of life.

J.M. Barrie, the author of *Peter Pan*, illustrates this point: *"Tink was not all bad: or, rather, she was all bad just now, but, on the other hand, sometimes she was all good. Fairies have to be one thing or the other, because being so small they unfortunately have room for one feeling only at a time."*

We are, fortunately, people, unlike fairies, and we can live quite peacefully with our human potential for expressing both strengths and weaknesses, even when those traits are on full display for others to evaluate. To achieve this goal, however, we must first accept that, because we can be neither good nor bad, we are rendered, by default, wholly un–ratable. We can fail and we can still live contentedly throughout our lives with the knowledge that we are never good or bad – only works in progress with a great deal of potential for both to exist in us at the same time.

* * * *

The all–good–or–all–bad rating system we now use is no more than a system of opinions. Opinions, however, are not often under our control, unless they are our own. In fact, if we base our human value on how we perform in relation to others, our value will always be a product of capricious and arbitrary opinion. The secret to self–appraisal, therefore, is to harmoniously coexist with all sorts of opinions, our own and those that are contrary to our own. Opinions can serve to give us information; but they cannot serve the purpose of defining our human value. Only we can do that, and our human value is always un-ratable.

* * * *

It seems the quickest way to defend against criticism is to invoke the protective shield of self–esteem to confidently deny that imperfection is or could ever be possible in one self. To maintain that grand illusion, we might resort to self-talk like, "I am beautiful and intelligent and no one can tell me different. If anyone does, they are wrong and should be damned. Not only that, but they are also quite jealous of me."

Aside from the fact that beauty and intelligence require that we compare ourselves to others to make those assessments, criticism doesn't necessarily have to be true or accurate. In fact, criticism doesn't even require the participation of another person. People often criticize themselves. The only requirement of criticism is that it holds some meaning and some value, a judgment of good or bad, in the mind of the person being criticized.

For example, someone may say that we behave like a melon or a pomegranate, and that evaluation would have little or no impact on our sense of ourselves and our own goodness. We would not be compelled to defend against these assessments. We might shrug it off as so much blabbering. On the other hand, we could be described as a big, fat pig and have an altogether different reaction based on the meaning we apply to that phrase. The point being that most people have not learned that being called a melon or a pomegranate is inappropriate or disagreeable and, therefore, would have limited potential for applying real or useful meaning to these words.

While people cannot be pomegranates or melons, neither can they be big, fat pigs; but we have learned that to be called a big fat pig holds a great deal more meaning than to be called a pomegranate.

＊＊＊＊

No event holds intrinsic meaning. All events are neutral and hold the precise meaning we apply to them. In fact, nothing happens that can be understood in only one way. There are always many, many options for the meaning we apply to the events we experience or that are within our perception. Being criticized is not a toxic event unto itself, unless we believe it is. It is how we view the act of criticism that will dictate how we will respond to it.

We all have weaknesses in our character, fallibility in our choices, flaws in our behavior and imperfections in our appearances. When these very–human blemishes are made more salient, we will respond, in some way, emotionally.

Our response to being negatively evaluated has a direct relationship to how clear we are about our own weaknesses and how much we depend on others for our intrinsic value. Are we truly conscious of our weaknesses, imperfections, limitations, faults and defects as integral parts of our natural human condition? Or do we pretend that we only behave ideally, precisely and are the model of perfection, the epitome of good choice, always worthy of emulation?

To adjust to criticism, and other opportunities for improvement, we must begin by recognizing our own propensity for being quite imperfect. We must start to recognize that to achieve a more reasonable standard of contentedness for ourselves we must first find true bliss in our imperfect selves.

* * * *

It is in our nature as human beings to fail, succeed, win, lose, come off well and behave badly. In that frame of mind, it should be no surprise to any of us when we experience this mixture of outcomes in how we encounter life. To develop a more accurate measure of ourselves, we must first change how we think about ourselves and our potential for imperfection. If we are postponing our contentedness, waiting for criticism to go extinct, we will likely live discontentedly for the rest of our days. We will likely not live as fully either, never taking a chance and risking disapproval.

If we take control of our thinking, we will make definite strides in how we address nearly any type of emotional adversity. We may start with our self-talk by repeating, until it overcomes what we tell ourselves now, *"The primary cause of discontent is never the situation but the thought about the situation. Be aware of the thoughts you are thinking. Separate them from the situation, which is always neutral. It is as it is."*

* * * *

Most theories that purport to explain emotion make a great deal out of self–esteem, ego–strength and similar concepts. After all, we are naturally–evaluating creatures, perpetually seeking to understand ourselves and our environment by placing things, including ourselves and others, into categories, good and bad, success and failure, triumph or defeat. When we go from evaluating our traits to equating that assessment to our view of ourselves and others, we go too far. There is more hope in maintaining a balanced self–image, one that recognizes our human potential for fallibility and our inability to be rated, using only one standard.

We may simply abandon the wilting concept of self–esteem and replace it with the idea of unconditional self– and other-acceptance. While a self–concept is believed to be vital for psychological health, self– and other-acceptance may hold the potential of being a more stable personality trait and a more useful social skill. People who practice self– and other-acceptance over self–esteem may begin to link their self– and other-awareness to what they and others are rather than what they and others do. You might begin to remind yourself: *I am human and my weaknesses do not surprise me. I can live contentedly with myself and my flaws. I can live contentedly with your flaws, as well.*

* * * *

Perfect is a 2010 song by Pink, an American singer–songwriter. The song follows the footsteps of *Raise Our Glass*, in terms of lyrical content and themes, purporting to encourage youth to seek a higher level of self–esteem, to view themselves as perfect, even if they fail in some way. Pink sings: *Pretty, pretty please, don't you ever, ever feel, like you're less than perfect.*

Unlike when I was a child, when adults freely and regularly criticized children and focused on making good boys and good girls of us, placing us in Murderers' Row and hiding us behind pianos (two very unlikely responses to bad behavior in our schools today), the pendulum has swung away. We now find every opportunity to praise our children, avoiding any suggestion that the child may not have succeeded, believing instead that the avoidance of critique and criticism is essential to healthy child development. Both approaches are extremes and inherently flawed. Neither approach represents the real world. A more balanced approach would be one where the potential for failure and success are expectations of life. We are never perfect. We are all works-in-progress. We all succeed and we all fail at various points in our lives, but we are never failures or successes. Even an Olympic gold medalist fails at something. Likely even on the same day s/he received h/er gold medal. We must train our children to make this fair and balanced self–evaluation for themselves, helping them to grow into more self–accepting, un–ratable, neither-good-nor-bad, adults.

As unfortunate as it may seem, we are not perfect. We were never intended to be perfect. We are, instead, perfectly imperfect. Perfection is a potential that humans cannot achieve. We are imperfect and un–ratable, neither good nor bad, neither a success nor a failure. Once we come to accept the perfect truth of our human imperfection, we will be closer to improving our emotional intelligence. It will take the force of will to do that.

Chapter Fifteen
The Chemicals Between Us

Our emotions are composed of a subjective component (how we think about our experiences), a physiological component (how our bodies respond to our thoughts) and an expressive component (how we behave in relation to our thinking). These three elements play an important role in how we achieve physical and psychological balance.

We all experience personal difficulties at some stage in our lives, events that can impact our quality of life and our ability to cope. When we are not in balance, stress, fatigue, emotional disturbance and interpersonal conflict may result.

Balance is the sense of being in control of one's life, one's responsibilities and one's destiny. When a person's existing schemas are capable of explaining and accommodating what is being perceived, s/he is believed to be in balance.

Of course, as we've already discovered, unless we are being chased by a hungry lion or hanging from a twig over the edge of a cliff, a majority of our psychological imbalance is a result of our thinking about the past and the future, the perception and the meaning we use to understand and address the unpleasant events we experience or have experienced in our lives.

Although the body responds to both real and imagined threats in much the same way, regardless of the legitimacy of the threat, I will invite you to stop reading now and assess the threats you face. If you truly are being chased by a black bear, I would recommend that you protect yourself, straightaway. If the threats you face are, instead, a product of your thinking, an invention of our mind, read on.

* * * *

We don't often think of blood, glands, neurochemicals, hormones and electricity when we think of emotional health. Emotional well–bring, however, is a delicate interplay of biological, psychological and social/environmental factors working independently and in partnership to produce our overall mental and physical health profile.

Emotional intelligence theory may be best understood as a multidimensional system encompassing not only thinking but also the body's physical response to thought. We call this whole-person view the bio–psycho–social (BPS) model. We might simply keep in mind, as we read through this section, that a person cannot have only one disease. Emotional problems interact with the body's functioning and often compromise the individual's physical health problems. Likewise, physical health problems can easily complicate emotional health. To treat only the physical problems, without recognizing the psychological corollaries, leaves the individual only partially treated and vulnerable to chronic disorder. This bio-psycho-social (BPS) theory of whole-person functioning may be described as follows:

The biological (bio) element of our emotional intelligence awareness is allied with the oft–overlooked anatomical influence on emotion, e.g., the limbic system (the emotional neighborhood), sympathetic and parasympathetic nervous systems, major organs, neurons and hormones.

The psychological (psycho) factor of our emotional intelligence/BPS awareness is aligned with rational emotive behavior theory (REBT) which endorses the application of rationality in personal decision–making, often citing Epictetus as its maxim: *What disturbs peoples' minds is not events but their judgments on events.*

The term irrational may be defined as dysfunctional thought processing that includes exaggeration, oversimplification, overgeneralization, illogic, unproven assumptions, faulty deductions and absolutistic notions.

The social (social/environmental) of our emotional intelligence/BPS awareness is related to the unique environments in which we are reared, i.e., family, community, state, country and so on, environments that greatly influence thought and encourage conformity in emotional behavior.

Rather than focusing only on thinking as the sole source of our emotional expression, emotional intelligence theory highlights the interchange between our thinking, our human anatomy and our social environment on the development and expression of our emotional behavior. Developing a keen insight into how our bodies interact with our minds may result in an efficient, flexible, open–minded and self–directed method for addressing our goal of improving our emotional intelligence.

* * * *

In today's healthcare environment there exists a hierarchically arranged system of care that is more focused on medical diagnosis, medical procedures and medications. This focus on the human organism, the physical body, as the primary target of treatment has both subordinated and weakened the need for what are believed to be less complex helping strategies, i.e., counseling, social work and psychosocial evaluations.

Somehow we have come to consider medical procedures to be superior to the types of care provided by practitioners of social and psychological interventions. Our emphasis on medical treatment over psychological and social services has resulted in a professional hierarchy favoring medical practitioners that leaves patients only partially treated. In that case, we may, as a primary skill for improving emotional intelligence, begin to view our own emotional and physical health in terms of having a strong relationship to one another, a combination of biological, psychological and social factors, rather than from a purely biological or purely psychological perspective.

Psycho–social conditions can instigate biological complications by predisposing the patient to unpredicted risk factors. Cancer, schizophrenia, diabetes, depression, anxiety or even a broken ankle are each best treated from a whole person perspective. For example, depression, by itself may not actually cause liver problems; but a depressed person may turn to alcohol and develop an addiction and suffer liver damage. Furthermore, it has been shown that Type–2 diabetes has a correlation to lifestyle choices, particularly food selections and physical inactivity. Without a complete assessment of a patient's way of life, medical and pharmaceutical interventions would only help to alleviate the biological component of the patient's illness and neglect to recognize or treat the contributing psychological factors resulting from every–day life.

Human biology and psychology do not exist separately. They are intimately engaged with one another, to the extent that one cannot be treated without exacerbating the other. Where a biological (physical) illness exists, there will likely always be a psychological and environmental corollary. Likewise, where there is a psychological illness, there will be a related biological response.

**** **

Most of us prefer to be in balance, a time when the biological, psychological and social components of ourselves are all working in harmony with one another, equilibrium, where our BPS system is stable, composed and neutral.

We might imagine balance as a deer grazing in a field, a layer of mist hovering over a still, tranquil pond, ducks flying overhead. Suddenly there comes a distant SNAP! of a twig. The deer freezes, pricks up its ears and tries to make sense of every sight and sound within its perception. The deer receives signals to its senses from all directions.

Its pupils dilate.

Its sense of smell becomes more acute.

Its hair stands on end.

The intense strength that may or may not be needed to fight or flee begins to gear up. Like fuel into a fuel tank, the animal's natural response to danger, its sympathetic nervous response, takes over and its bloodstream is suddenly flooded with adrenaline, cortisol and norepinephrine, the three essential hormones necessary to propel the animal to safety, if need be.

The fight–or–flight–or–freeze (FF&F) response is a physiological reaction that occurs in response to a perceived or imagined harmful event, attack or threat to survival. Animals react to threats with a general discharge to the sympathetic nervous system, priming the animal for fighting, fleeing or freezing. More specifically, the adrenal medulla produces a hormonal cascade that results in the secretion of catecholamine. This response is recognized as the first stage of a general adaptation syndrome that regulates stress responses among vertebrates and other organisms.

The human FF&F response, like the deer, is intended to protect us from all types of peril, threats of peril or anticipated peril.

Only, with humans, those threats are not limited to threats of physical harm. Humans process what might be termed psychological harm (social threat) through the same system of self–preservation and protection (physical threat). Essentially, we might talk badly to a deer and not make any impression at all, while humans will respond to ridicule, criticism, judgment and disrespect in much the same way as a deer responds to the SNAP! of a twig in the wood.

To a far greater extent than in other animals, human social behavior has evolved significantly over time. The FF&F response, however, has remained virtually unchanged and continues to resemble that of our most primitive human relatives.

Where thousands of years ago the FF&F response was essential to our human survival, we now use it primarily for an entirely different purpose. What worked for humans at the dawn of time to protect us from being eaten by a threatening predator may not be as helpful for that purpose, today. The threats to our safety have significantly decreased over time, and our need to protect ourselves against predators has become less and less necessary. Our FF&F response (what we now refer to as our stress response) has never completely forgotten its evolutionary roots. Time has not altered our human blueprint for self–preservation, leaving us with little skill for distinguishing between threats to our lives and emotional threats to our ego and our self–image.

It appears that modern humankind often confuses a rude, uncooperative person with a hungry black bear. To our primitive, un-evolved stress response, criticism and black bears are identical. Our minds only have to perceive danger or imbalance, to activate the stress response.

Ideally, considering the numbers of years humans have roamed the planet, it seems we would have, by now, when confronted with an emotional issue, evolved some system that relied on our intellect to recognize that emotional confrontation is not the same as a physical threat to our very lives. But humans have not evolved in this sense and are programmed in much the same way as their oldest ancestors to fight, run or freeze when they perceive danger, emotional, physical or otherwise. Like hearing a twig SNAP! our thoughts over a disagreement with another person will prepare our bodies automatically for hostility, menace and danger.

"I have to disagree with you. I think you are wrong."

"Well, if I'm wrong, you're stupid."

"You can't say that to me."

"Sure I can. I just did."

"Why you! I'll show you!"

"Bring it."

The threats we encounter in our daily lives are menaces to our minds. Much like being chased by a lion (or a wild and wooly, groundhog) judgments of our character, assaults on our values, morals, principles and standards, slights to our appearance, snubs about our child's school performance, a slur about our mothers are all emotional threats; our twig SNAPS! setting off an alarm to protect us from a perceived danger.

"May I help you?"

"I need to return this cleaver."

"Do you have a receipt?"

"No, I lost it."

"We don't take returns without a receipt."

"It's the wrong size."

"I'm sorry I can't help you."

"You're not really sorry."

"Yes I am."

"What do you expect me to do with it?!"

"That's your option. We cannot take it back without a receipt."

"It's my option? Are you getting smart with me?"

(Staring at each other.)

(Silence)

"How about I shove it up our ass? Is that one of my options?"

"Security!"

* * * *

Stress is a merged, finely–tuned BPS response, activated by thought more often when we encounter something we determine to be a threat, real or imagined. Stressful thoughts can result from such things as taking an examination, divorce, death of loved one, moving or losing a job. Often, if we tell ourselves certain activating thoughts, we can expect an increased heart rate, shallow breathing, a decrease in digestive activity and a release of glucose for energy. We can also expect a sudden rush of catecholamine into our bloodstream. The decision to activate the stress response is made by the brain and is directly influenced by the input it receives from our perception and thinking. Depending on the meaning we apply to the events we experience, we can expect a corresponding release of stress hormones to sustain our attempt to fight or flee the thing we believe will harm us.

"You're rude."

"That's your opinion."

"You're an asshole!"

"Prove it!"

* * * *

Often we don't realize we're in the middle of stress until we're in the middle of stress. By then, the stress hormones that power the stress response are in our bloodstream and are influencing our thinking and our judgment. If our body is flooded with stress hormones, as a result of our thinking, it will respond to those hormones, leaving us nearly powerless to the strength of the body's own drive to survive.

* * * *

Thought is the brain's way of accessing experience (perception) as a tool for understanding one's environment, how one is trained to respond to h/er own particular culture. Thought activates a part of the brain (the limbic system) and does one of two things: maintains homeostasis (balance) or activates a protective response (fight/flight/freeze).

Our own innate warning system triggered much like the deer in the meadow that hears the sound a distant SNAP! can be triggered through thought, imagination, memory and perception. Thought can initiate a sudden burst of neurochemicals and hormones intended to sustain our efforts to survive, priming us for fighting, fleeing or freezing. For instance, imagine that you're on the phone with our doctor's office. You have been placed on hold and forgotten. You wait and wait and wait. Finally, the receptionist returns to your call and asks if she can help. "I've been waiting for fifteen minutes," you say. Your heart is beating rapidly. You feel yourself beginning to sweat.

You hear, "How can I help you?"

You feel yourself beginning to shake (adrenaline and norepinephrine are entering our bloodstream and circulating through our viscera. Your heart is responding). Your voice rises. "I already told you I wanted to make an appointment to see the doctor," you hear yourself saying. (Sustaining the thoughts that prompted the stress response continues to pump more and more adrenaline and norepinephrine through your body.)

You hear, "No need to get angry. Name?"

The hair on the back of our neck seems to stand on end. (This is Nature's way of preparing us to cool our skin as we progress toward our ultimate decision to fight or flee.) You say, "My name? I already gave you my name! Fifteen minutes ago, I gave you my name!"

You hear, "Ma'am, you will have to give us your name again, if you want to receive help."

You feel your whole body shaking (adrenaline with nowhere to go) as you slam the phone into its holder. For a few minutes you cannot think clearly or stop shaking. (Nature doesn't give the human organism the freedom to think rationally when the body believes it is being attacked by a wild animal.)

After a few minutes, however, the chemicals you produced to fight the imaginary threat to your life have begun to dissipate. You call your sister and tell her what happened, "What would you have done? How would you have responded? Was I right?"

"Yes, you were damn right!"

"I felt like killing her."

"You were right. She was an asshole."

You suddenly feel relieved, another chemical process. Safe and approved of, your body releases an endorphin called dopamine, a comforting reward from Nature for having survived the threat that never really was a threat at all.

As previously mentioned, perception and thought activate the very same stress response used by our oldest ancestors to protect them from real physical harm. We might get chased by a dog, or have a bird land on our head, but actual physical threats in nature are not common. The threats we are more likely to encounter include fear of the unknown, inconsiderate people, trying to control destiny, traffic jams, the loss of friends and family and hopelessness.

* * * *

The body's stress-response system is usually self-limiting. Once a perceived threat has passed, hormone levels return to normal. As adrenaline and cortisol levels drop, our heart rate and blood pressure return to baseline levels, and other systems resume their regular activities. But when stressful thinking is constant, ever-present and we constantly feel under attack, also known as chronic stress, that stress reaction stays turned on. The long-term activation of the stress-response, and the subsequent overexposure to cortisol and other stress hormones, can disrupt almost all our body's processes, placing us at increased risk of numerous health problems, including:

*. Anxiety

*.Depression

*. Digestive problems

*. Heart disease

*. Sleep problems

*. Weight gain

*.Memory and concentration impairment

If we want to improve our emotional intelligence and, thereby, reduce the number of occasions we rely on our stress response to reconcile the adversity we encounter in our lives, we will have to learn to control the switch that activates the entire process – thinking.

Of course, if we really are being chased by a wild, hungry and aggressive goat, we should do our best to use every bit of our FF&F response to escape to safety. But the events in our lives that we perceive as threats, those that are not truly threats at all but are, instead, inconveniences, hassles and annoyances must be reconciled differently, if we want to remain balanced, physically and emotionally healthy.

* * * *

Emotionally intelligent people know that thinking and perception (and, therefore, the stress response) can, with practice, be more under our own personal control. To believe that we are under the control of others is to believe in magic. If we want to emote differently, and take control of our stress response, it may be logical to assume that we have to think differently.

Surrendering personal control over our own thoughts is to make us vulnerable to an overreliance on the stress response to reconcile social and emotional problems. That idea can only lead to discontent and physical disease. Intellectual insight or the ability to understand the concepts we discussed may be the easier challenge to improvement in our emotional intelligence. Behavior change, on the other hand, in relation to what we are coming to know and believe, is an altogether different and more time-consuming goal. Simply, it isn't enough to know, we must also do.

* * * *

The amount of time it will take to realize some level of improvement in our emotional intelligence is proportionate to how willing we are to commit to behavior change. There is also a correlation to improved emotional intelligence and how long we have trained our minds to believe our emotions are under the magical control of other people.

Infants, children and young adults, on up to twenty-five years of age, are likely to make quicker gains in achieving improvement in emotional intelligence. Their brains are more receptive to changes and new ideas. For the rest of us, we might begin to consider how skilled we are at recognizing self–defeating thought; how well we can accept the idea that we are responsible for our own emotional health and, finally, how well we can merge our new thinking with novel, more self-enhancing behaviors.

We must become aware that we feel negative, self-defeating emotion, for example, because we think in terms of how awful, horrible and ghastly we are being treated by others or how our life is progressing. It's not surprising that, in response to these thoughts, one can expect that stress hormones will not be far behind. To change one's emotions, to return the body to its primary objective which is to be in balance, we must change the way we perceive and think about events and, to the best of our ability, through better thinking, prevent the flow of stress hormones into our bodies.

* * * *

It is not uncommon to hear the phrase, "She pisses me off!" If we believe that we are being pissed off by something outside our control, we will automatically relinquish our responsibility to ourselves to control how we perceive what we experience and, instead, initiate our stress response in an effort to protect ourselves from the perceived dangers we associate with being pissed off.

Emotionally intelligent people must, to make headway in achieving a personally defined measure of emotional wellness, commit to living in a world where, although most people believe they can be pissed off by someone else, refuse to buy in to the idea that others are not responsible for our feelings. This type of thinking not only makes life more bearable, but also reduces the stress hormones we would have otherwise produced through demanding and damning others for not behaving as we believe they should.

* * * *

If we believe our emotions are the product of how we are being treated, we relinquish control of our feelings to something external of us. If we do that, we will likely have to postpone our own contentedness until people begin to behave the way we demand that they behave. That can take a lifetime or, more likely, never at all. It may not, therefore, be the best option to believe that our contentedness depends on how others behave.

We must not lose sight of the contributions we make to our own state of mind through our own thinking. We may, instead, maintain our authority over our own contentment. We can be content, even while living in a world where people behave as goodly or badly as they choose.

Each of us has within us a deep longing for everything to be put right, to be in balance. So our minds and our bodies will actively attempt to cope with emotional challenges, expending the energy necessary to meet that demand. Once the threat to our balance is overcome, we are expected to resume our lives in peace, until the next short–term challenge to our balance presents itself. A steady diet of long–term stress, however, without the requisite period of emotional and physical rest and relaxation, places an unusual burden on our capacity to rebound. Nature never intended the stress response to last as long as we often sustain it in modern times.

* * * *

We have only one system for responding to threat, and it has not adapted well to our contemporary demands. Somehow Nature has allowed social and physical threat to coexist as a single unit. This is the cycle in which most of us engage the world. Our human biology, our human psychology and our social environments all work together to produce and sustain our emotional health. We must use these systems more effectively, to achieve better outcomes in our goal for improved emotional intelligence. It will take the force of will to do that it.

Chapter Sixteen
Come On, Get Content!

Our emotional intelligence may improve the more we practice new ways of thinking. Only we, however, will know if we've achieved our goal. If we're seeking to just tweak our emotional intelligence, or if we are planning a complete overhaul, it may be a tough slog either way. There are often years upon years, layers of self–defeating thinking and perceiving to wade through to accommodate a more self–improving frame of mind. If that were not enough, the world is jam–packed with those who would have us return to our former way of thinking. We grow accustomed to believing that we make others feel, and vice-versa, and they will not likely stop reminding us of this magical idea and invite us back into the fold. You will discover, after practicing your new language, that emotionally intelligent people don't talk like the rest of us:

"You made me so angry!"

"I did nothing of the kind."

"You are obstinate."

"How is that a problem for you?"

"You should take responsibility for how you make me feel."

"It's hard enough for me to take responsibility for how I make myself feel."

"I think you're insane."

"I think I can live contentedly with your opinion."

* * * *

Although the words *happiness* and *contentment* may seem identical; there is a distinct difference between them. Happiness may be described as an emotional *response* resulting from an event. Contentment, by contrast, may be described as a temperate, moderate managed emotional *state*.

It may be that contentment is more enduring than feelings of happiness. Essentially, we can be happy some of the time; but we can be content all of the time.

Happiness comes from the Norse word *hap*, meaning *luck* or *chance*. *Glück* in German can be translated as either happiness or chance, while the Greek word for happiness, *eftihia*, is derived from *ef*, meaning good and *tixi*, luck or chance. Contentment is derived from the Latin *contentus* and is translated as being *satisfied*.

The paradox of hedonism, also called the pleasure paradox, refers to the practical difficulties encountered in the pursuit of pleasure or happiness. Happiness-seeking may not yield the most actual benefit in the long run, for consciously pursuing pleasure interferes with experiencing it.

Feelings of happiness are the product of episodic, short-term occurrences that provide only fleeting benefit, something like a drug, leaving the individual empty without a continued source of happiness to improve their state of mind. Contentment may, on the other hand, reference a deep-seated, abiding acceptance of oneself and the worth of others resulting in a sense of meaning and purpose without continued, external stimulation.

Acceptance is the key to contentment. We must learn to accept everything we experience as if we had asked for it ourselves. Whether we like it or we don't cannot be the first question we ask ourselves. It is what it is and liking or disliking contributes nothing to the reality that it is.

Resistance of what is creates two difficulties from one. Not only do we have the situation we are facing, but we now have our resistance to the situation to contend with.

While contentment is the product of acceptance, it isn't an excuse to surrender to it, although surrender is an option. We may mistakenly think that acceptance is a resignation of one's goals and ambitions. On the contrary, contentment is a process of making peace with what is and, by doing so, agreeing that change is possible.

For example, I did not realize that I would grow old. Once that reality became harder to avoid, I resisted, and still slightly resist it. The reality that I am growing older is showing on my face. Even to admit this is a little difficult for me. It is a fact, however, that impacts every other area of my life and will for the rest of my life. Rather than pushing against this truth, I can accept it, fully appreciate the progress of my life and life in general. Or, I can live in denial of it, which usually expresses itself in the continuation of those behaviors that have resulted in my fear of aging. Acceptance may move me toward a better appreciation for the aging person and health, nutrition and psychological well-being.

* * * *

Few people are encouraged to take an honest and true accounting of their physical, mental, emotional and spiritual strengths and weaknesses and derive contentment from that assessment. Instead, we set out to achieve goals that are designed not around our capabilities, but, instead, to validate our worth as human beings. Each time we flop, we believe we are worthless; each time we win we are winners. Our sense of happiness, thereby, is only as enduring as our last achievement.

As an alternative to viewing ourselves fairly and objectively, contentedness, we seek to achieve a kind of happiness derived from the full use of our ambitions to seek happiness:

If we graduate from college, we will be successful and live our lives happily. If we don't, well, we will not be happy.

*. If we are gay, we will never be happy. We couldn't possibly be content living with that much ridicule and shame.

*. If we make thousands upon thousands of dollars, we will be happy. If we make less than that, well, we will be less successful than others and, by that, we wouldn't be happy.

*. If we fail, we will be a failure and no one will ever view us as a serious person. We couldn't possibly ever be happy.

* * * *

We may begin to build our definition of contentedness by truly and honestly assessing our strengths and weaknesses and establishing a balanced view of our own true, human potential. We are not perfect and we were never intended to be perfect. We have weaknesses and we have strengths. We may remove from our definition of contentedness such things as material wealth, power and parade floats. If we are not enough without these three very common inhibitions to contentedness, we will not be enough if or when we achieve them.

It will not be easy to develop a personal definition of contentedness. Like everything related to improved emotional intelligence, however, we will have to work at it. It will take the force of will to do that.

Chapter Seventeen
Honorable Beliefs

People typically acquire their emotional behavior through what we might call emotional programming, repetitive exposure to the affective and behavioral traditions appropriate to the society in which they were raised. To a large extent, just as we learn to speak language, choose certain foods over others, commit to memory the rules of driving and the practice of religion, our emotional choices are developed through coaching and repetition, forming the framework of our present emotional range. Simply said, people within the same family, neighborhood, community, city, town and state teach each other how to encounter emotional events. Very little is random; nearly all of our emotional routine is learned. That being the case, nearly all of it can also be unlearned.

At some point, however, without some motivating reason to do something different, people eventually leave their homes and go off into the world, expressing emotion similar to those with whom we socialized throughout our early life – free to teach their children the same emotional customs they were taught. Problems often arise when we meet people who were raised from a different emotional and behavioral custom, sometimes making compromise quite difficult. Emotional conflict often results.

As I mentioned in previous chapters, shit happens and we do the same things we've always done when we encounter it in the world, especially when we encounter adversity and resistance to our demands. Improvement in emotional intelligence means that we recognize the source of our emotions and the weaknesses we've acquired over time in our thinking and behaving and we commit to doing something else.

Children can be a powerful source for witnessing social-emotional education in action. Children are wired for learning and their every-day behavior can be a means of discovering how we establish the framework for resolving emotional issues later in life. For instance, a young child, new to a grocery store, is suddenly immersed in a wonderland of novel colors, smells and sounds. The child may believe s/he has entered the *Willy Wonka Candy Company*, surrounded by lollipops, chocolate bars, cakes and cookies. Of course, before the child even entered the grocery store, s/he already possessed a number of skills for getting what s/he wants. For the sake of making this explanation simpler and easier to follow, however, we will pretend s/he hasn't prepared in any way for the experience.

The child begins by reaching for the colorful treats. If the child doesn't get what s/he wants, s/he will reach again and possibly add a disturbing grunt or whine. If that doesn't work, the child may reach, whine and scream. After a few unsuccessful attempts at using these behaviors, the child may escalate and create a unique combination of reaching, whining, kicking, hitting and screaming fashioned in a way to more forcefully get the caregiver's attention and to gain h/er cooperation at meeting h/er demands. The caregiver at this point has one of two choices, to give in to the child's demands or to allow the child's behavior to escalate and then to go extinct.

If the child is rewarded with the treat after perfecting h/er collection of cohesive, demanding behaviors, s/he will likely begin at that precise point next time s/he wants something, having learned that other, less volatile behaviors don't work. Why not just cut to the chase and start where s/he knows h/er behaviors do work in achieving h/er goals?

On the other hand, if the child, instead of getting what s/he is reaching for, gets no response at all, the child will realize, at some point, that no behavior will get h/er what s/he is seeking and that when the caregiver says, *No*, s/he really does means *No*.

The simple fact is all behavior has to have a purpose. People will not behave in ways that do not bring them some kind of reward. If behavior does not bring a desired result, behavior will go extinct.

Extinction is a process of ignoring behavior, forcing it to die away, encouraging alternative activities that are more along the line of acquiring an increased aptitude for frustration tolerance. It is best, therefore, not to allow the process to get underway, to begin with. Once it is started, it is much more difficult to reverse.

The acquisition of social skill is so important to human survival Nature leaves the initial process of acquiring emotional custom on–going for the first 25–or–so years of human life. It is not unusual to see a seventeen-year-old behaving as if s/he were a five-year-old. The seventeen-year-old is still in a stage of neural development where testing behaviors and logging information related to experience is still an active process. As we grow older, we don't just suddenly stop behaving like a child to get what we want. If we were allowed to behave inconsiderately, explosively, and thoughtlessly in childhood and into early adulthood, we can expect that as we mature we will just perfect these goal-seeking behaviors and become whiny, demanding, self-centered and needy adults.

* * * *

The human brain does not reach full maturity under age twenty five. After twenty five years of logging social-emotional information our brains seem to settle in on a routine for encountering the world, and we are not so welcoming of changing what we have grown accustomed to thinking and doing. As the years progress, people will actually react forcefully against change that requires even the slightest modification in thinking and behaving. In fact, people will defend their premise for expressing a particular thought and emotion at a particular time with a great deal of fervor, even if they know it isn't bringing good results. Fortunately we can change our behavior, with effort, regardless of our age, and we can be successful. It just becomes more and more difficult as the years progress.

Even we as adults may still be reaching, whining, kicking and hitting to get what we want, especially when we encounter people who refuse to cooperate and are resistant to our demands. Our demandingness of ourselves and others may be what prompted us to improve our emotional intelligence in the first place.

* Do we find ourselves seeking perfection in our own behavior?
* Do we find ourselves making ourselves angry and depressed because others resist our demands and expectations of them?
* Do we find ourselves making ourselves discontented when people don't act perfectly?

Adults, like children, will have to be encouraged to give up their self-defeating thinking and behaving and replace it with something that brings a more rewarding result. The reward we may be seeking at this point is a stable, more manageable emotional life. In that case, there may be many years of learning to overcome.

* * * *

Emotional change requires a mixture of new thinking and new actions the individual is willing to practice in place of h/er undesired behavior. For example, if we want to quit smoking, we are not likely to replace smoking with peeling potatoes. In order to change behavior, we must be willing to replace the undesired behavior with one that we believe is a compelling substitute. People have to like the alternative to what they want to stop doing. The same can be said for emotional change. We have to want to be less stressed, more composed and saner than we are at the moment, to be motivated to seek to improve our emotional intelligence. We will have to want emotional well-being more than we want to live with emotional instability.

* * * *

Thought and behavior change require us to challenge long-established beliefs, customs and rituals of thinking and behaving that are passed on to us by those who raised us. We might call these social-emotional customs our *honorable beliefs*. For example, ideas about patriotism, religion, politeness, gender roles, sexual behavior and even what we eat and drink on Friday can make up a portion of our honorable beliefs, passed down to us through our encounters with others. To question the validity of holding some of the ideas we hold may be perceived as a compromise in our relationships with our parents, grandparents, neighbors, church leaders, heroes and mentors. People will seek a great deal of evidence to defy the ideas that were given to them by such an esteemed and honorable group of educators.

Our honorable beliefs are made up of such things as what we believe *should, ought, must, has to* and *needs* to happen in order for us to be happy in our lives. What we will call our absolute musts. Improving our emotional intelligence will depend on our application of the very best definition and purpose we can establish for using absolute musts to navigate our emotional life.

Absolute musts are the beliefs we hold, the emotional customs, rituals and traditions related to how we learned to interact with others, as we are growing and developing. We learned that in relation to our absolute musts, there is simply no wiggle room, no chance for mistake or free will. For instance, we may hold the following absolute musts:

* We must be polite.
* We must be helpful.
* We must be respected.
* We must never lie or be lied to.
* We must conform.

People often believe, on some level, that they should have absolute control over themselves and their environments. When we don't, we will likely be frustrated and experience fear and tension. The use of absolute musts in how we encounter the world contributes to a large extent to how we resolve our emotional problems. The following describes this frustration-disturbance process:

* We perceive that when we can't have what we want when we want it, and we believe we absolutely should, ought, must, have

to and need to have it when we need it, we make ourselves frustrated and anxious.

* We tell ourselves that we can't stand it when we don't get what we believe we absolutely should, ought, must, have to and need to have and begin a process of self-talk that includes those words, thereby decreasing, rather than improving, our frustration-tolerance.

* We repeat these messages over and over in our heads and become fixated on the idea that we not experience frustration and that we absolutely should, ought, must, have to and need to be free of discomfort in our lives in order to be content.

* We preoccupy ourselves with these thoughts and limit our opportunities to consider more life-enhancing alternatives, impeding improvement in our emotional intelligence.

I encourage my reader to be very familiar with how s/he uses these terms and how these ideas can have a great deal of potential to interfere with emotional problem-solving and improved emotional intelligence. When we use these words and phrases, we are declaring our unalterable demand for perfection and our intolerance of variation from ourselves and others.

****

Absolute musts are inflexible models of behavior that most of us respect, but often fall short of achieving, ourselves. No one, including you, can live h/er entire lives in an ideal state. Make a lot of room for imperfection by curbing or even eliminating the words should, ought, must, have to and need from our vocabulary and our emotional intelligence may likely grow by leaps and bounds.

* * * *

It may be best to develop new ways of expressing our ideals (our honorable beliefs) possibly by making inflexible declarations more into statements of personal preference. "We should not behave that way and I can't stand it when we do," can become, "I would prefer that we behave differently, but I can stand it when we behave badly." In addition, "I need you to treat me respectfully," can become, "I would like you to treat me more respectfully, but I can live my life without your cooperation."

Using absolute musts not only denies the possibility for fallibility in ourselves and others, but also denies the fact that others often make unintentional mistakes or simply exercise their free will to make choices and behave any way they choose.

If we would like to make an immediate improvement in our emotional intelligence, we may begin by replacing our absolute musts with the terms *prefer*, *want* and *would like*; words that make our demand for how others must behave more flexible, realistic and less stress-provoking.

* We can perceive that when we can't have what we want, it is not essential to our contentedness to get it. In this way, we make ourselves, at most, sad that we don't get what we want, but it is not the end of the world.

* We can tell ourselves that we can stand it when we don't get what we want and begin, instead, a process of self-talk that includes such words and phrases as would like, want and prefer, thereby increasing, rather than decreasing, our frustration-tolerance.

* We can change our self-defeating self-talk by repeating these rational messages over and over in our heads and become fixed, instead, on the idea that we will likely experience frustration in our lives and that our lives will never be entirely free of discomfort. Discomfort is a likelihood of human life and it is best to develop strategies for acknowledging and remembering that.

* We can begin to practice these new thoughts and, thereby, improve our opportunities for more life-enhancing thinking and behaving, resulting in an improvement in our emotional intelligence.

* * * *

I often find my clients saying they are content with their absolute musts and choose to hold on to them. It's likely because they consider their beliefs in how people should behave to be quite moral, decent and fair. There is something to that. The key, however, is that absolute musts are inflexible, dogmatic and not useful with fallible human beings. The absolute musts we declare for how everyone should behave in relation to us are not even possible for ourselves, all of the time. So, by that standard, when we demand (rather than hope) that others behave according to our absolute musts, we go too far. We cannot hold others to an unalterable standard of behavior if we do not always meet that standard ourselves.

Our honorable beliefs are the standards we will use one day to judge the merits of our culture. But, in the meantime, to improve our emotional intelligence, we will have to modify our strictly held beliefs so that they both honor the best potentials of human behavior, but also recognize the reality that people will not always live by or even accept our beliefs, no matter how much we think they should. We might begin to change our self-talk. We might say, "I like it when people treat each other with respect, but when they don't, I can still live with it. I will never like it, but it is not awful or horrible and I certainly can stand it."

We might also say, "I can be sad that people are disrespectful. I will never like it, but I can remain content when it happens. I can treat others with respect, regardless of the way people choose to behave toward me. It will be hard to do, but so is improving my emotional intelligence." It will take the force of will to do that.

Chapter Eighteen
Rules of the Road

If we're looking for a classroom, somewhere to practice our ABCs, to have an *in vivo* (in life) learning adventure, look no further than our own windshield. People who drive cars are not always following anything more than their own rules for driving; much like the way we live our lives. Through the windshield of our cars, we can be alone with our thoughts and breathe in the challenges to the emotional imbalance unfolding before us.

Most of us have an emotional response to people who travel the highway in the passing lane, the left lane, oblivious to those behind them who want to pass. *You're not supposed to be in this lane! Don't you know the rules? You should be damned for traveling in the passing lane! Everyone knows the rules. Why don't you? I'll show you. I'll tailgate you until you submit to my superior driving intellect and my authority! I know tailgating is against the rules; but this is different. You must be trained in how to behave! And I must train you!*

With a clear path to pass on the right, many of us will stay firmly affixed to the bumper of the guy in front of us, determined to teach him to follow the rules. If the car moves to the right and allows us to pass, we feel vindicated for being treated in such an ill–mannered fashion, although we might give a scolding glance as we pass (or a firm hand gesture). We might even feel less angry, considering the driver did get out of our way and, of course, is now more redeemable.

If the car doesn't move, we will continue to tell ourselves that the ruthless villain (idiot, asshole) should behave more courteously, lawfully, considerately and thoughtfully. This emotional mess will continue for a while, until someone gets bored and makes a move to resolve it. Often it is us who will simply decide to pass on the right. *What an idiot! What a complete asshole! He's not following the rules. I hope he crashes into a tree! That'll teach 'em!*

This analogy can be easily applied to our daily, non–driving emotional challenges. When we have a difference of opinion with someone, when people treat us poorly or with disrespect, when others won't cooperate with what we believe they should be doing, we have a choice. We can tailgate them until they change their view, making

197

ourselves miserable in the process, making ourselves intent on being inflexible and stubborn; or we can just pass on the right. We can smile and wave on our way by, and we can thank them for the lesson they provided us. *We–hoo! Thank you for the learning opportunity!* It's up to you.

* * * *

Most days, I set off in my car and I don't bother wearing a seat belt. In fact, I am quite intent against seat belts. I don't like how they feel. I find them confining. Instead, I freely arrange myself in my seat, turn on NPR, take a deep breath and embark on my commute. I am well–prepared for anyone who would intentionally or unintentionally interfere with me. I almost never use a turn signal and I only half–yield at yield signs and only half–stop at stop signs. (I can tell if the coast is clear when I am approaching these signs, so there is really no need to stop or yield, completely.) I'm a very good driver.

If I stop to turn right on red, I normally stop in the cross walk, or in the middle of an intersection when the traffic is heavy. When I am well–merged and soaring toward my destination, I make telephone calls, drive over the speed limit and check what's left of my hair in the visor mirror. For the record, I never shout at pedestrians or other motorists (like my sister does) and I most certainly would never use hand gestures to emphasize or articulate my position on an issue with another driver. Most of the time, in fact, I don't really believe the rules of driving apply to me at all. I am a smart person, and a very safe driver, without having to pay strict attention to the rules.

Unlike those for whom the rules were correctly and most competently written, it is my burden, instead, to endure the idiocy of other motorists, each of whom would most assuredly benefit from a driving lesson from me. To cope with it all, I talk to myself. *You idiot! What in hell are you doing! How dare you do that to me! You are rude and I cannot have that! You will pay for that move, my friend.*

Only when I am provoked, and my fight–or–flight (stress) response is activated, will my mind override my limbs and I suddenly find myself assertively posturing my shiny ego car against the recklessness and stupidity of others, maneuvering in such a way as to register my displeasure. In all fairness, I wouldn't dream of using my horn for anything except to provide a little nudge when someone in front of me is too slow to respond to a green light. A toot, if you will – a matter of doing my part to maintain the even flow of traffic.

Driving here and there, up and down, to and fro, is all a straightforward matter of collaboration and cooperation. (There is an element of copulation as well; but we won't go there.) Knowing the basic ABCs is where driver-awareness might result in improved emotional intelligence. Identifying self–defeating thoughts (self–talk) that are rigid, extreme, unrealistic, illogical and absolutist, while in the safety of our cars, is a grand opportunity for improving our emotional intelligence while, at the same time, refining our driving skills.

While driving, when we find ourselves in a traffic problem with another driver, or in a jam or simply when there is an obstruction to our course, if we are able to identify our self–talk (beliefs) and chart it within the ABC paradigm (in our mind of course), we will have a starting point for forcefully and actively questioning and disputing our self-talk, replacing it with a new emotional language; a language that is more adaptive to more stable mental health and safer driving. Try it! The road will provide us with more challenges to our emotional problem solving skills than we can imagine.

* * * *

It took a while for me to apply the ABCs to my own life, to the point where it made only a modicum of difference. Today it's how I try to live my entire life and how I encounter challenges to my emotional intelligence. But in the beginning, I only knew what the ABCs were meant to represent. I just met an array of unexpected challenges when I tried to use them. The following strategies are imparted from my early experience using the ABCs to improve my emotional intelligence and may help reduce the amount of time we spend learning, using and understanding the paradigm:

STRATEGY ONE: Not every negative human emotion is self–defeating and worth examining with the ABCs. Just because we're making ourselves uncomfortable does not mean it has to be run through the ABCs. Sometimes it is easier and more efficient to live with the inconvenience than to exhaust ourselves trying to eliminate all forms of bother. Instead, we might just want to try to improve our frustration tolerance. Endure it. We cannot live in a hassle-free world. Be a candidate for the change we hope for in others.

STRATEGY TWO: An emotion must be unmanageable to process it through the ABCs. Anger can take on unmanageable proportions, but not all anger is a candidate for the ABCs. Some anger is very manageable, somewhat motivating and often quickly dissipates. Some forms of love are unmanageable. If we are expressing obsessive love, it may be time to work through that issue. It can easily become unmanageable anger. Regardless, it is important to know that when we use the ABCs, we focus on the unmanageability of emotion, not the elimination of emotion from our lives.

STRATEGY THREE: It is not our goal to become emotionless. Emotion is an essential part of our human existence. It might be our goal, instead, to celebrate our unique character and the array of emotional experiences we can have with others. We can and should celebrate all that we are, emotionally, if we are to achieve a fulfilling and complete life. Ridding ourselves of emotion is not our goal. Nor is it possible, without surgery or trauma. And even then it is a precarious operation. Managing unmanageable emotions is our goal. Celebrate our emotional beauty! Try not to make our emotional sameness with others the standard by which we judge ourselves. Enjoy ourselves and learn to forgive ourselves, regularly.

STRATEGY FOUR: It takes dedication to get the most out of the ABC system. The paradigm will make sense at face value if we look it over, it doesn't take a long time to conceptualize it. The practice of the ABCs, however, is the tough part. Think about the years upon years we've spent developing our roles and scripts. We've spent many, many years learning to play roles and to recite scripts for nearly any emotional situation we encounter. We have to rid ourselves of those roles and scripts that are harmful, unhealthy and self–defeating. We can replace them with more manageable, rational and flexible thoughts and behaviors.

STRATEGY FIVE: It's as if there are containers of dusty roles and scripts floating round in our head. We can imagine throwing a match on them and watching them go up in flames. That can be our sign that we have to start to build new ones. If we don't practice, if we fall back into our old emotional language, we won't achieve our desired results. Changing the way we think and behave will be the most important thing we can do to build our emotional strength. The more we practice, the more energy we dedicate to delivering healthier emotional information to our brain, the closer we will get to our preferred result.

STRATEGY SIX: It takes patience to achieve our new emotional milestones. Don't beat ourselves up when we fail at achieving our improved emotional intelligence. Our skills with the ABCs cannot be developed quickly or immediately. We have to commit to achieving results over the long haul. Quick fixes never work, so don't expect any. It takes a plan, dedication, and proper attitude to get the results that we are looking for. Without the personal commitment to the task, we'll give up before we reach our goal. Be diligent, focused and patient. With the proper dedication and the right attitude, which is the best way to build our emotional intelligence, we will make steady recognizable progress to reaching our mental health goals.

****

I am not a big fan of measuring emotional intelligence with anything but one's own individual desire to improve and the awareness that one has or has not improved. The concept of emotional intelligence, however, appears to be acquiring a commercial edge.

We can be tested for our level of emotional intelligence for a price. Our emotional intelligence, however, is really up to us to decide. If we think we could profit from examining our emotional intelligence, so be it. Our previous discussion of driving and its value in gauging our level of emotional intelligence may come in handy as we determine our own personal level of improvement without the use of testing instruments. What does our driving personality tell us about ourselves? We might pay close attention to our thoughts and behaviors while behind the wheel and make a judgment of how much improvement we might need in our emotional intelligence by way of that experience, alone.

That's just one way of making an assessment of our emotional intelligence. We may also find ourselves arguing more than we would like. We may find that our stress response is in overdrive and won't seem to allow us to relax. In fact, there are a number of signs and signals that improvement in our emotional intelligence may be necessary to sustain not only our emotional health but our physical health, as well.

* How do we reconcile a disagreement with a coworker?

* How do we accommodate people who we believe are being discourteous?

* How well do we follow the rules that we think everyone else should follow?

* How are we at conforming to impediments to our goals?

* Has our thinking and behaving become a pattern where people must cooperate with us for us to have continued contentedness?

We may find that our answers to these questions will closely approximate how well we regulate our thinking and our behavior in our waking and walking life. Are we willing to express patience, tolerance or pity for those we encounter who disagree with us, impede our way or behave counter to our expectations? When people make errors that affect us, are we quick to label them bad, wicked, evil or depraved? Do we provide ourselves with enough evidence to determine that someone is inferior, purely on the basis of one or more of the poor choices they've made? When people act objectionably, do we reconcile ourselves by conjuring in our own mind their true intention? Do we ask?

Go for a drive.

Find a congested area.

If we like how we behave, so be it.

If we don't, we can change it.

Imagine greater.

It will take the force of will to do that.

Chapter Nineteen
Who's Betty?

I often tell my clients that the toughest feature of trying to live sanely and rationally is the idea that most people believe *they* and others *make* people feel emotion. As if we lived in a culture of magicians and sorcerers. The fact is, people perceive what others do and say and they make judgments about those behaviors. They think about them, and they generate an emotion that they believe is supportive of their judgment.

If we choose to forgive or pardon people for their poor choices, rather than ranting and raving about the injustice of it all, we will not express unmanaged anger and be more likely to express managed displeasure, discomfort and discontent. In that frame of mind, we are more likely to express our disapproval and be heard. Generation after generation we teach our children that their emotions come from the way other people treat them. They learn from the start to attribute their feelings to things outside of themselves. Under these circumstances, launching a new mindset, after years and years of training, is made so much more difficult. Changing the shape of the human mind is less painful when it is fresh and more impressionable.

If we have children, we might begin to use the lessons in this book to start our child's emotional training. We might begin by helping them learn to take ownership of their emotions. I remember working with a woman, employing the skills we are discussing. She had a very young son, and started teaching him her new–found philosophy very early. "Mommy didn't make you discontented. We make ourselves discontented. We can't always get our own way. We can be patient instead. We can make a better choice. What better choice could we have made?"

We may be thinking, "How can a child understand these concepts?" Well, it's easy. Children have to hear the concepts from you and they will begin to assimilate them into the way they think and feel. Just like the way they hear the nutty ideas we teach them now. Over time, this philosophy can become the framework from which children understand their world.

Once my friend's child started first grade, all was well; until his teacher said, "You shouldn't do that! You are a bad boy! Bad!" to which the child replied, "I am not a bad boy. I made a poor choice. I will try to make a better choice next time."

We are wired to adapt to emotional challenges, at any age, through repeated experience and social learning. Nature makes it inevitable that we will learn to cooperate, if not simply for survival. Our goal to improve our emotional intelligence, however, is not to adapt to society's prevailing opinion. It is to act against it, when to comply would bring unhealthy results.

Our challenge then will be to improve our emotional intelligence while living in a world where most people reject the idea that they create their own feelings. As we try to change and maintain our new internal logic, we will still have to go to work, shop, interact with people at the movie theatre and drive a car, making the process bewildering and often lonely. I am reminded of a time when I was leaving a meeting and a woman stopped me to tell me how I made her so angry.

"Goodness, how?" I asked.

"You disagreed with me," she said, "On that issue about healthcare."

"That *made* you angry?"

"Of course it did. I think my position was very clear. How would you feel?"

As I listened to her, I imagined myself unmaking her anger, waving a magic wand over her head and making her content again. For, wouldn't it be logical to think that if I could *make* her angry, I could also *make* her content? "I guess I could have agreed with you, instead," I said.

"Yes, you also embarrassed me."

"The extent of my power over you is unsettling."

"What?"

"I'm sorry."

We must interact with misinformed people, people who think we make them feel, and we must try to talk like them, if we want to get along. But, once we begin to make improvement in our emotional intelligence, never again think like them!

Sadly, the more we improve our emotional intelligence, and the saner we become, we still have to live in close quarters with the misinformed. They own most everything, they are often the objects of our affection and they are decidedly in control of much of the world's food supply. So we should learn to appease them, at every turn, to survive. Here is the social survival script we may want to learn, but never believe: *I'm sorry to make you discontented. I'm sorry to make you angry. I'm sorry to make you feel anything but contentedness. Your emotions are my burden in life. Your emotions are my responsibility. I promise to handle your emotions more delicately in the future and provide you with ample opportunity for contentedness, even if it means I will have to be discontent to make that happen.*

* * * *

It's hard to say how many magical, externally focused concepts have been allowed to flourish within our culture, our language and ostensibly, our species. It could be that our ancestors needed a certain level of illogical thinking and behaving to achieve cooperation within a tribe. Regardless of the reason, we speak to one another, live with one another and cooperate with one another in a way that accommodates insanity.

* * * *

Yesterday, while in the men's room, I noticed a lot of dried mud on the floor. It appeared that whoever had previously used the commode had obviously ridden motocross and then cleaned his shoes where I was sitting. I contemplated the dirt, myself. The redness of the clay–like quality interested me. (One of the pieces of muck looked a lot like Abraham Lincoln.) On my way back to my office, I saw one of the janitors lingering in a corner by the stairwell. I told her of the dirt on the bathroom floor. After returning to my office, I soon forgot about it, losing myself in my work. That afternoon, one of the secretaries in my department came to my cube. "Can I talk to you about something?"

"Yes, come in," I said, motioning her to sit.

The woman stood before me, hands clasped. She said, "Would you please apologize to Betty?"

"Who's Betty?"

"She's one of the ladies who cleans up. The janitor–lady."

"Why on earth would I apologize to Betty?"

"For the mess you made in the bathroom."

I stared for a moment, "I didn't make the mess. I reported it," I said.

"She's all tore up about the mess. She had to sweep it up and mop the floor. She had to take an emergency smoke break. She's as mad as a bee. You really made her mad."

"Did I?"

"Why won't you just apologize? You'd make her feel a lot better if you did."

Later that day, I found myself staring into Betty's tear-filled eyes. I hesitated a bit, but I was determined to use my new social survival script and just make it all go away. The words started flowing. "I'm sorry I made you unhappy," I said, placing my hand on her shoulder.

It took the force of will to do that.

Chapter Twenty
Emotional Distance

My third and final therapist, a psychologist, was in his late fifties, bald, casually dressed. Walking into his office was like waking up in the lower drawer of a dusty filing cabinet. There were books, magazines and yellowed paper scattered everywhere. "You're looking for an REBT therapist, eh?" he responded to my question about my preference. "Have a seat." He moved a pile of newspapers off the chair, across from the couch where he would sit. He took a half–eaten apple off the coffee table and tossed it by its withered stem into the wastebasket, "Here, sit." A Brussels griffon jumped into my seat and began licking its paws. I looked at the therapist and, ever so faintly, smiled. "Just shoo him off. Shoo," he said. He fanned his yellow legal pad at him. The Brussels jumped down and ran behind the gray, metal desk. "How can I help you?" He looked at his watch. "Two–thirty," he said.

"I am a student and I have to do 10, I mean 4 hours of therapy as a client. I've already finished six of them." I reached out my therapy log for him to initial, "I wanted to work with someone who knows REBT."

He took the tattered therapy log and tossed it onto his disordered desk, "OK, then. What's on our mind?"

"I'm bald."

"How is that a problem for you?"

"I look old?"

"What does it mean about you to look old?"

"It means I'm ugly." I paused, waiting for him to take exception with that assessment.

He didn't. He just trotted ahead, "And if you're viewed as ugly, what does that mean about you?"

"It means no one will think I am attractive."

"And if no one thinks you're attractive?"

"Well, no one will care about me."

"It's quite unlikely that would happen, but what would it mean if no one cared about you?"

"It would mean I don't deserve to be loved. It would mean I was unlovable."

Suddenly he slammed his hands on the arms of the tattered couch, "All of this from being bald? Are you nuts? You need a therapist!"

"I guess," I said, actually interested in what had just happened.

"Well, at least you can agree on one thing." He leaned in toward me. "Do you want to stop being nuts?" He then proceeded to tell me that my emotional reaction to going bald was really a matter of the value I placed on other people's opinions of me. My emotional reaction to my hair loss had little to do with baldness and had everything to do with what I was telling myself about it.

"What do you tell yourself about losing your hair?"

"Well that no one will want to date me if I'm bald."

"And what would that mean about you?"

"That I am worthless, I guess."

"Kid, if it weren't our baldness, it would be something else. If you all of a sudden sprouted a new head of hair, you would find something else to condemn yourself about. It isn't your hair that you're worrying yourself about. It is ridicule, plain and simple. You're afraid of being viewed as flawed and imperfect. Let's work on that and leave this foolishness with our hair out of it."

My new therapist told me, in so many words, if I continued to depend on other people for my personal value, I would never view myself as suitable for anyone's affection. "People might complain about your eye color, your education, your weight, your breath, the shape of your ass. We will never be satisfied until we are perfect." The Brussels jumped onto his lap and he petted its caramel–colored fur. I cupped my hand over my mouth and blew into it, trying to smell my own breath. He continued, "It will all end when you understand that you have value as a human being without hair. Hell, you could lose both your ears and still retain your intrinsic human value. Your problem has nothing at all to do with your hair. We have to help you change the thoughts you have about not being perfect."

Here was another person telling me that my emotions originated in my thinking. All of a sudden, I was back in Chicago with Al. There was no escaping it. My emotions come from how I perceive how people interact with me; not how they speak to me; not how they behave toward me. My interpretation causes me to feel an emotion. To get better, I would have to pay less attention to what people thought of me and more to what I thought about myself.

* * * *

Frequently, when people experience psychological hardship, they find themselves trying to solve their emotional problems inside their own head. Thinking, endlessly reviewing the same information, looping into the same emotionally charged result, never really resolving anything. Just like using only thought to find a solution to a complicated math problem, trying to solve a complicated emotional problem within the confines of our own mind may be just as elusive. Staying focused is often a challenge, and complex problems are better understood by drawing on our total competencies.

Many of us are at a loss when we find there is no one to talk with about what is concerning us. When something happens, and we have thoughts that disrupt our emotional stability, our balance, we might call a friend, a family member or, if things are really out of control, we might make an appointment with a therapist. While we wait for the return phone call, we sit and think, summoning the problem to mind, rolling it over and over in our own minds, and waiting for someone to reach out to us.

To talk.

Something we might think of doing to improve our emotional intelligence is to change who we turn to for help. Add a new dimension to our thinking and behaving. Turn to ourselves. We can become an active part of our own emotional life. We can talk to ourselves, using the ABCs, especially the disputation (D) phase of the paradigm.

We don't ordinarily think about ourselves as a mental health resource, when we have a problem. As a matter of fact, discussing our emotional issues with ourselves would probably rank last in the list of potential collaborators, rivaling the discussions we have with our dogs. After all, isn't talking to oneself a sign of mental illness? We allow ourselves the comfort of speaking to ourselves when we want to remember a series of numbers, the directions to the main road or a list of items we need from the grocery store. We sing to the radio, and hope no one hears us making up the words. We can have elaborate discussions with our deceased relatives, but we can never experience ourselves in that same manner. Somehow we learn that we must keep an emotional distance from ourselves.

We seem to be in contempt of our own guidance. To achieve the highest benefit from this program, however, it's time to start depending on ourselves and our own best advice.

Risk is a good thing in behavior change. Nothing changes without some level of risk. We have to take risk to escape the status quo. After all, it is our embrace of the status quo that has prevented us from achieving improved emotional intelligence. Begin a relationship with ourselves by saying out loud: *Hello! I have been with you my entire life and I have never once introduced myself to you. I am pleased to know you and I can't wait to share my thoughts and ideas with you. We know each other pretty well, already. Just by sharing experiences. You are really the only one I can truly trust and who knows me. Let's make a plan to talk every day. Maybe on the way home from work, in the car. That way we can be alone, and we won't have to think about anything else.*

Listen to our own voice. Talk to yourself about the ABCs. Learn how to dispute out loud. Learn the voice of your teacher. The voice of your true best friend. It will take the force of will to do that.

Conclusion

This book has offered no magical elixirs or ethereal philosophy that will resolve your issues with your mother or overeating or tell us why people treat us badly. It does contain good, practical solutions and easy–to–learn methods that, if we choose, will bring about immense change in your life.

You were introduced to emotional problem-solving skills that will come in handy if you find yourself relapsing, reverting back to your old ways of thinking and behaving.

People who are treated for emotional concerns, after a period of wellness, think they are cured for life. Consequently, when they slip back into old habits, and discover their old problems are still present to some degree, they are likely to despair and give up working on themselves altogether. Oftentimes, when relapse is likely, people will return to therapy. This book, however, promotes not only self–efficacy, but also a new way of living using a more effective method of emotional management.

I believe that people are better prepared for life when they learn to take greater responsibility for their own personal growth and change – not when they develop a dependency on pills and therapists to help resolve their emotional issues.

You will be expected to practice your new–found skills independently for the rest of your life! At times, the statements I've made and the solutions I have suggested may be hard to incorporate into your daily life. After all, you have been living your life a certain way using your own thinking and reasoning skills for, well, your whole life. Changing the way you think, behave and, ultimately, live your life will take a great deal of courage and strength.

You will have to commit to that goal.

* * * *

The little girl from my elementary school just may have been responsible for me spending much of my academic life trying to understand the substance of emotion. I write this book with her smile fixed in mind.

I carried her note in my back pocket, untouched, until after school. When the bell rang, I took off across the ball field. The dugout was the most private place I could find. The note was folded into some sort of box shape, and I was careful not to tear it, treating it as if it were a map to a secret pirate treasure. I finally got it unraveled and I remember smirking at her good penmanship. The note read: *Do your homework!* She had drawn little smiley faces into each of the Os.

Of course, we were in love from that point on. We never spoke a word to each other; but each time I turned in my homework, and each time it was returned with a passing grade, I looked at her and she at me and we both smiled.

Life changed for me after that. I was paroled from Murderers' Row and allowed to roam among the living.

The rest is history.

So, for the little girl at South Elementary School, Holbrook, Massachusetts, this book promotes the use of homework as a vital part of the process of improving emotional intelligence. Our homework should consist of one or more self–directed activities, designed to encourage us to independently act against how we traditionally respond to adversity. Our homework should result in some level of change to our thoughts and behaviors. For instance, if we fear a certain social activity, we might intentionally place ourselves in the feared social situation. While immersed in the activity, we will be ready to address our thoughts in relation to that situation. That way, we will be aware, in real–time, of what we tell ourselves, how we thwart our own ambitions and how to work through them. I can only say that the suggestions I have made to help improve our emotional intelligence will work if we let them; if we do our homework.

I cannot promise that there will never come a time in your emotional life that you won't ever make yourself feel miserable again, no matter how much you take away from your reading. On the contrary, you will feel every single emotion you have ever felt before reading this book. Only now you will celebrate anger, sadness, irritability, resentment and annoyance. You will view these as opportunities for learning, rather than setbacks. With practice and patience, with homework, you can develop alternative methods for overcoming emotional hardship, by reaching an emotional resolution that suits your personal goal of contentedness and, of course, by sucking a lemon and tasting a cinnamon jellybean.

It will take the force of will to do that.

52018594R00137

Made in the USA
Middletown, DE
06 July 2019